TABLETOP
FOUNTAINS

TABLETOP
FOUNTAINS

Easy and
Great-Looking
Projects
to Make

DAWN CUSICK

LARK BOOKS

ASHEVILLE, NORTH CAROLINA

ART DIRECTOR
Celia Naranjo
PHOTOGRAPHER
Evan Bracken, Light Reflections
ILLUSTRATOR
James True
PRODUCTION ASSISTANT
Hannes Charen
ASSISTANT EDITORS
Heather S. Smith
Catharine Sutherland
PROOFREADER
Julie Brown

Library of Congress Cataloging-in-Publication Data

Cusick, Dawn.
    Tabletop fountains : easy and great-looking projects to make /
Dawn Cusick.
        p. cm.
    Includes index.
    ISBN 1-57990-105-0
    1. Tabletop fountains. I. Title.
TT899.74.C87 1999
745.593—dc21   99-30747
                                                                CIP

10 9 8 7 6 5 4 3 2 1

First Edition

Published by Lark Books
50 College St.
Asheville, NC 28801, US

© 1999, Lark Books

For information about distribution in the U.S., Canada,
the U.K., Europe, and Asia, call Lark books at 828-253-0467.

Distributed in Australia by Capricorn Link (Australia) Pty Ltd.,
P.O. Box 6651, Baulkham Hills Business Centre, NSW 2153, Australia

Distributed in New Zealand by Southern Publishers Group,
22 Burleigh St., Grafton, Auckland, NZ

Printed in the United States.

Acknowledgments

Many thanks to everyone who contributed to the preparation of this book.

LOCATION PHOTOGRAPHY
Chris Bryant, Constance and John Daly, Rob Pulleyn, Deitra Saunders, and Terry Taylor.

TECHNICAL INFORMATION AND SUPPLIES
Robin Clark of Robin's Wood in Asheville, North Carolina for woodworking assistance;
Cynthia Gillooly of the Golden Cricket floral shop in Asheville, North Carolina for
lending vases and vessels; Larrisa Gleason at Beckett Corporation in Irving, Texas for
submersible pump information and samples; and Larry Steeves of Raka, Inc.
in Delray Beach, Florida for epoxy information and samples.

NETWORKING AND SUPPORT
Carol Taylor, Deborah Morgenthal, Danielle Truscott Dawson, Heather S. Smith,
Catharine Sutherland, and St. Jude.

"*Ideas for fountains are everywhere. I have a million ideas.*"

—Susan Kieffer
Fountain Designer

Contents

Introduction   10

Fountain Basics   12

    The Mechanics   14

    Design Accents & Concealers   18

    Play Time   22

    Preparing Materials   25

    Basic Assembly   29

    Dealing with Details   24

    Preventing Problems   35

The Projects   36

Contributing Designers   127

Index   128

Introduction

For centuries people have marvelled at the wonders of moving water. Perhaps it's the soothing sound. Or the wonderful patterns formed by diverted water flows. Or maybe it's just the idea of taming something so critical to life. Whatever the reason, fountains have played an important role in the lives of people all over the world for centuries.

The earliest documented fountains date back to 4000 B.C. in Iran where ceramic remains suggest they were part of garden water designs. Western fountain traditions are thought to have originated in Greece, with both archeological remains and carvings in vases serving as evidence. These early fountains simply diverted natural springs. It wasn't until centuries later that public fountains were constructed to serve as municipal water sources. Many cultures utilized these functional fountains as decorative displays as well. The Romans, for example, incorporated carvings and statues into their public fountains, and the private homes of many wealthy Pompeii residents had courtyard fountains.

Renaissance fountains were marked by their elaborate architectural designs. Circular and polygonal shapes were popular, as was sculptural detailing. Ornamental fountains served as focal points for government buildings and royal palaces, creating dramatic water displays that required substantial engineering skills. Although most fountains were now purely decorative, folklore from around the world continued to hold that water could be blessed with the power to renew the spirit, preserve youth, and restore life. Inhabitants of the Bahama Islands told Spanish explorer Juan Ponce De Leon about a fountain of youth whose waters had brought vitality to an elderly man. In 1513, Ponce De Leon discovered a well-established Native American settlement in North America built around a spring many believed was this elusive "fountain of youth." The spring has been walled up to make a fountain, on display at The Fountain of Youth National Archeological Park in St. Augustine, Florida (pictured here).

Architectural fountains have enjoyed cycles of renewed interest over the last hundred years. Between 1910 and 1930, dozens of dazzling fountains were built throughout the United States as part of the City Beautiful project.

The rising popularity of indoor fountains is an unexplained phenomenon. Perhaps indoor fountains are the natural link between outdoor and indoor spaces, and their popularity is tied to rising interests

in gardening. Or perhaps water is the newest material for sculptural artists and interior designers always in search of the newest trend. Or perhaps tabletop fountains are just our way of celebrating our collective past, of bringing a piece of the grand and the historical into our homes in a very downscaled, manageable way. Whatever the reason, tabletop fountains are sure to become even more popular as home crafters discover the joy of making and living with indoor fountains.

Tabletop fountains are a great way to quell interior design boredom— just exchange out the bowls or change the rocks. You'll get a whole new look without the sore

back that comes from moving furniture. If you make the fountain on page 55, for instance, and tire of looking at water flowing over mementos from your last beach trip, just unplug the fountain, replace the old items with new ones, and you'll have a new fountain up and running in less time than it takes to bake a pan of muffins. Most of the fountains in this book are also lightweight enough to move from room to room as your whim dictates. Expecting company? Move your coffee table fountain to a dresser in your guest bedroom. Want a special centerpiece? Move your small window fountain to your dining table? Tired of a table fountain? Purchase a tall plant stand and lower the fountain into it.

There tend to be two types of fountain makers. Those who are materials driven: "I love those mini tea cups...how can I make water flow in and around them in a fountain?" And those who are more project driven: "A fountain on the left side of my coffee table would be great, but it needs to match the throw pillows on the couch and silk flowers in nearby vase." As long as you end up with fountains you love, either process is fine. This book will help you discover that building fountains is easy. And fun. Learning how to choose the materials that go into a fountain and fine-tune the placement of those materials, though, can be challenging and takes some practice. Just remember: anything that won't dissolve in water is fair game. Finding materials for tabletop fountains is like going on the world's best scavenger hunt. Keep your sense of adventure close at hand as you build and design your fountains—it will serve you well.

Fountain Basics

*T*here are two main goals that need to be in the forefront of any fountain maker's mind. First, always cover the mechanics of the pump. Second, create an eye-pleasing design. Sometimes you can kill both birds with one stone, as in the fountain shown at left. Other times, as in the fountain shown at right, the pump is hidden with one set of materials and the design is created with another.

THE MECHANICS

Virtually every fountain—no matter how expensive, elaborate, or decorative—can be broken down into just a few critical parts: the pump, the water conduit (usually plastic tubing), and the water basin. Anything else you see in a fountain is there for the purpose of disguising these parts or enhancing the overall design.

Pumps

Every fountain begins with a pump. There's simply no way around it. Once you've adjusted to that fact, you'll be pleasantly surprised at how user friendly they are. Submersible pumps are small, simple, and reasonably priced (less than dinner for two at a nice restaurant). They work by pulling water in through an intake filter and pumping it up and out an opening. Since this process defies the laws of nature—gravity, in particular—the pump requires electricity as an energy source.

Submersible pumps are the mainstay of every fountain. Look for them in garden supply shops and larger craft stores.

Submersible pumps can be found in many garden supply shops and in larger craft stores. Several features are important and can affect price. First, how high will the pump shoot water? The higher the shoot, the greater the cost. Since most indoor fountains are fairly small, there's no reason to spend the extra money on a pump that will shoot water 20' (6 m) in the air. The smallest pump available will work just fine.

Second, notice the length of the cord. A short cord (12" or .3 m) really limits where you can display your finished fountain. Three to 5' (.9 to 1.5 m) is a much more versatile length. (Note: Unlike most other small electrical items, the cord

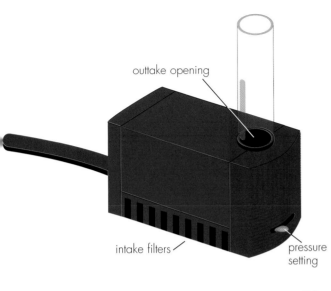

outtake opening

intake filters

pressure setting

on a submersible pump is not replace-able—doing so would destroy the cord's waterproof seal—so you can't purchase a short-corded pump with the intention of adding length at home.

Third, note where the water pressure switch is located. (Most pumps have two, if not more, different pressure set-tings.) Some brands locate the switch on the electrical cord, instead of on the pump itself. In most fountains it doesn't matter where the switch is located, but if you're making a fountain in which the pump is difficult or impossible to access after a certain assembly stage, hav-ing the switch on the cord is a wonderful feature.

Water Conduits

Plastic tubing is used to move the water from the pump to the area you want it. Tubing can be found wher-ever pumps are sold, as well as in the aquarium section of larger pet stores and in hardware stores. Many pumps do not give required tubing sizes, so you may need to bring your pump with you when you shop for tubing. It's generally very inexpensive and can be easily cut down to any length with a utility knife or sharp scissors.

Plastic tubing inserts easily into the pump's adapter and then runs water to anywhere you like in your fountain.

You may wish to experiment with different widths of tubing. Generally, the narrower the tubing, the greater the force that will be exerted on the water, so the higher the stream. Adapters that bridge the seam between two pieces of different sized tubing can be found in many auto supply stores.

Keep an open mind when choosing a fountain basin. Many containers that you might be quick to eliminate can be waterproofed with sealants or liners.

Basins, Bowls, and Other Containers

There's a world of great containers out there, in all sorts of surprising places, just waiting to be discovered. Larger garden stores offer an amazing variety of containers and other design elements, many of them with predrilled holes designed especially for fountain making. Antique stores, specialty stores, and even your local discount store can also stock a wealth of supplies.

When shopping for interesting basins, try not to rule something out just because it isn't waterproof. (See page 25 for waterproofing techniques.) After you've found a good container, search the aisles of a large garden section for a protective plastic liner that fits fairly well inside it. If you can't find a plastic liner that fits, look in the kitchen section of a large discount store. Clear plastic salad bowls and other serving dishes also make great liners; they're inexpensive and come in a wide variety of sizes and shapes.

Water

Perhaps the most taken-for-granted fountain material is water. What would any fountain be without it? Normal tap water (if your local water isn't too hard) or bottled water are the best choices. If your muse tempts you to replace the water in your fountain with some clever alternative—champagne and bubble bath, for example—control yourself until you can test your prospective liquid's pH. Liquids that are too acidic or too basic can weaken the pump's seals and will eventually ruin the pump.

A submersible pump will reward you with years of spectacular water displays if you treat it with care.

To test a liquid, purchase a pH test kit (often available where pool supplies are sold) and follow the manufacturer's instructions. Only liquids with pH readings between 5 and 9 are safe to use in your fountain. (Champagne and bubble bath, by the way, do not pass the test.) These tests are simple and quick to perform, and are well worth the extra effort when you consider the expense of damages. Some additions, such as food coloring, do not change the pH of the water and can be safely used if desired.

Tame an overzealous water flow by placing a marble or bead over the outtake area.

Another water consideration is temperature. For proper flow, fountain pumps need to be used in water between 32 and 98 degrees F (0–37° C). Keep in mind that water will freeze below 32 degrees, which can cause the pump's motor to burn out. Extreme temperatures can also weaken the seals in the pump, and tight seals are crucial for good pump performance.

DESIGN ACCENTS AND CONCEALERS

Design accents are materials that help create the ambiance and "world" of the fountain, while concealers are objects that creatively hide the pump and any related mechanics (such as tubing or piping). When design accents and concealers are well chosen and arranged, even the most analytical minds won't be tempted to mentally deconstruct the fountain.

Design Inspirations

Design elements in fountains do so much more than just look pretty. They actually serve as clever ways to disguise the mechanical elements mentioned above. A good fountain should look as though the flowing water is completely natural, and design elements help do that. Virtually anything that won't dissolve in water and can withstand the pressure of having a hole drilled through it for tubing is fair game. Pretend you're going on the world's best scavenger hunt. Use your imagination and your sense of adventure.

Bring your sense of adventure and your Cinderella spirit with you when shopping for design materials. Anything that can be drilled, angled, polished, or spray painted is fair game for a fountain.

Stones and Rocks

Stones and rocks work well as both accents and concealers. The natural variations in their sizes and shapes allow for easy and flexible maneuvering—they can be built around virtually any pump, or simply scattered around a finished fountain as last-minute natural touches. Don't limit yourself to what's in your back yard when in need of stones and rocks. Garden centers, gem shops, and aquarium shops often have unusual selections. When shopping for special rocks, look for crystal formations, natural weathering, and veins of secondary minerals that add visual interest. If you've narrowed it down to two or three types of rock and you're having trouble deciding, pour a few drops of water over them and compare the changes. Some rocks just glimmer when wet, while others look exactly the same.

Top Row Left: Most garden shops offer an incredible variety of stones and rocks, many of them tumbled to enhance colors and patterns. Center: Consider giving your stones a quick makeover with a coat of polyurethane. Right: A visit to a gem or rock shop can spur ideas for dozens of fountains. Bottom Row Left: Marble scraps are a great material choice for covering mechanics. Center: Stacks of slate make a lovely, natural touch to any fountain as well as providing a nice surface for water to spill over. Right: Volcanic rocks, available where many outdoor fountain materials are sold, make a good rock choice when you're trying to minimize weight. They also—reputedly—serve as natural water filters.

If you will be purchasing special rocks for a fountain, build the fountain with ordinary yard rocks first, then disassemble the fountain and bring the rocks shopping with you so you'll have a fairly accurate idea of how many rocks to buy. In many fountain designs, only the top layer of rocks shows in the finished fountain. For these fountains, it makes sense to use ordinary, inexpensive rocks in the under layers to minimize expenses.

Marbles and Other Glass Gems

Marbles make wonderful concealers: they're colorful, reflective, and glimmer like jewels when in water. Antique marbles can often be found at yard sales and in antique stores, while newer marbles can be found in any number of sizes and colors in larger gift and toy stores. Glass stones, which look like flattened marbles, make good substitutes. Look for them in craft stores and in the aquarium section of pet stores.

Above: Available in a multitude of colors and sizes, marbles and glass gems stones make wonderful additions to fountains, either to fill awkward gaps or to fill an entire bowl. Right: Multicolored glass shards that have been tumbled until their edges are smooth are available in many craft supply stores.

Plants

Water and plants are a natural combination. You can purchase small aquatic plants at larger garden centers or in the aquarium section of pet stores. Another option is to create a fountain design with room for small plant containers. Just be sure that you choose plants that will thrive in a high-moisture, low-soil environment.

Many plants thrive in the moist environment created by a misting fountain.

Air plants are a great way to add natural greenery to your fountains. Because they don't require soil, you'll never have problems with potting soil clouding up your water or clogging your pump's filters. These exotic plants from the Tillandsia family originated in the West Indies and the Americas. Most varieties bloom in the spring or late fall and require occasional waterings (about once a week) and feedings. Be sure to request care information at the time of purchase.

Small assemblages of slate, stones, and air plants make lovely design additions to fountains.

PLAY TIME

Now that you're familiar with all of the parts of a fountain, the best way to proceed is to spend some time playing. Investing just 30 minutes doing the exercises below and then another 30 minutes studying the illustrations in the next section will transform you from novice fountain maker to a confident fountain designer. It's that simple.

Start with a kitchen sink full of an assortment of dishes (dirty or otherwise). Stack the plates on the bottom, largest ones first, then add progressively smaller dishes to the pile. Place a bowl on top of the plates. Turn on the water and watch how it spills down the sides of the plates. Shift the water flow so that it falls into the bowl. Watch as the water spills over the sides of the bowl and then over the plates.

Place a small cup inside the bowl. Shift the water flow into the cup and watch as the water fills up the cup, then spills into the bowl, fills it up, spills onto the top plate, and then finally spills over the sides of the plate. Continue playing in the sink for another few minutes, adding new dishes and utensils to the pile to create new water flows. Pour yourself a cup of hot coffee or tea and keep watching.

The next step is to fine-tune your fountain-building skills. Note that you'll be doing the same basic thing as in the paragraph above, but the materials you'll be using will give you more control in how and where the water will flow. (In fountain making, more control equals more creativity.) Assemble the materials below on a newspaper-lined surface in your kitchen. Cut the foam into a variety of shapes and sizes. At this point, there aren't any wrong ways to assemble a fountain. The goal is to play and learn, not to create great art. Pretend you're back in kindergarten.

MATERIALS

- Submersible pump
- 8" (20 cm) length of plastic tubing
- Block of craft foam
- Serrated knife

- Pointed object such as a sharpened pencil or a screwdriver
- Large mixing bowl
- Playful, relaxed attitude*

*Note: This is not the step to do with an audience. Send all highly opinionated neighbors home to play in their own sinks.

A variety of foam shapes allows you to play with the effects of varying shape and water flow in fountain design.

Use a twisting motion to make a hole through each of your shapes. Vary the location of the holes, putting some in the center, some in a corner, and some in the middle of a side edge. Put the mixing bowl in your sink and place the submersible pump inside it. Note the location of the pump's intake filters and add enough water to the bowl to completely cover them by at least an inch (2.5 cm). Gently work the electrical cord out of the bowl and over to a socket. Stand aside and plug it in. (Obviously, dry hands are a good idea.) Study the water flow. If you didn't step aside fast enough, change out of your wet clothes and return to the kitchen a wiser fountain maker.

Unplug the pump and adjust the pressure setting. Stand aside again and plug in the pump. Note the difference in water flow. (If you still haven't mastered the standing aside part, remain in your wet clothes: they'll serve as a good reminder.) Unplug the pump again.

Insert one end of the plastic tubing into the pump's outtake adapter. Choose several pieces of foam and thread the tubing through their holes. Slide the foam pieces down the tubing until they rest on top of the pump. Stand aside and plug in the pump. Watch how the water flows down and around the shapes. Readjust the pressure setting and notice the differences. Unplug the pump when you get bored. Assemble a new selection of foam blocks into a stack. Note the effects of changing sizes, arrangements, and hole alignments.

Chop one of your foam blocks into ½" (13 mm) squares and use these squares to add space between your foam blocks. The more space, the more distance the water will "fall" from one block to another. Slide your favorite foam block arrangement down over the plastic tubing and experiment with varying amounts of space. Plug in the pump and play some more. As you're playing, imagine that your foam blocks are any number of other fountain materials: slate, tile, decorative pots, dishes, etc.

Silly? Perhaps, but good fountain designers allow themselves to think of virtually everything as potential design materials.

Continue playing for a while, then start looking around your kitchen for additional materials. Choose something from your fruit bowl—an apple would work well—and twist a hole through it. Thread the apple down the tubing. Look through your cupboards for something with preexisting holes—a colander or a grater maybe—and thread it down the tubing. (Yes, this is getting silly, but once you've made a fountain out of an apple and a grater, you can make a fountain out of anything.) Now look around your house with a critical eye. If you find yourself saying, "That cobalt bottle would be gorgeous in a fountain if it just had a hole in the bottom," then you're on the right track. If you didn't find at least five things around your home that would look great in your fountain if only they had a hole in them, then return to the sink and take another look at the grater with an apple on it.

Preparing Materials

Once inspiration for a fountain strikes, you may have difficulty forcing yourself to spend time doing anything other than assembling the fountain. And while the process of preparing materials can seem like a tedious waste of time that's sapping your creative juices, you may find that this time is an opportunity to fine-tune your design plan.

Waterproofing

The first step in making any fountain is to test your basin for waterproofness.

Place the basin in your shower and fill it with water. Watch the basin for 24 hours, looking for both blatant leakage and subtle seepage. Solve major leakage problems with the purchase of a plastic liner; solve less disastrous leakage problems by first caulking the seams with silicone and then coating with several layers of waterproofing varnish or sealant. Alternatively, many materials can be soaked in commercial water-seal products. Refer to the manufacturer's instructions for specific how-to details.

A variety of water sealant products are available to help you protect fountain materials from water damage and leaking.

The ability to waterproof fountain materials adds a new dimension of design possibilities. Wonderful craft techniques, such as polymer clay, paper collage, and tole painting, can be used to create materials for distinctive, one-of-a-kind fountains if they've been carefully waterproofed.

Drilling

Although you can make many wonderful fountains without ever drilling the first hole, there's a good chance that some day a fountain you really want to make will require picking up a drill. And while working a drill does take some specific knowledge, it's nowhere near as difficult as learning another language or calculating a tax depreciation schedule. Relax.

For best results, you'll need a variable speed drill, not a cordless. (More control equals less breakage.) Bits, which actually make the hole, fit into the drill. They come in many different sizes (both metric and fractional) and are sold both singly and in sets. It's important to purchase a bit designed especially for the material you're drilling. If you're drilling a piece of tile, for instance, you should use a glass and tile bit. Other common bits include masonry bits, wood bits, and metal bits.

Protective eyewear should always be worn, no matter how simple the drilling job or how rushed you feel. Broken drill bits are easy to replace at the local hardware store—damaged corneas are not.

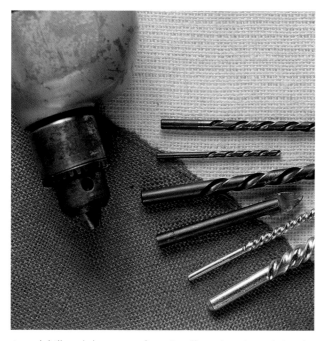

A good drill can help you transform virtually any item into a design element for a fountain. A contemporary teapot with fine lines? No problem. Just be sure to work slowly and carefully, following all safety and manufacturer's guidelines.

There's an infrequent, but painful element to drilling that needs to be kept in mind. Sometimes the pressure of the drill bit can cause the item to crack. If you're drilling an ordinary piece of garden rock, this is not a great loss. But if you're drilling a one-of-a kind, dear-to-your-heart, or cost-a-pretty-penny item, breakage can be very unpleasant. Although you can't prevent drilling disasters, you can minimize them by following the steps below. If your item isn't too expensive, you might want to purchase a spare or two. (Extras can be returned later if you're lucky enough not to need them.) For more expensive items, your best bet is to drill something very similar as a test. Some breaks can be repaired with a strong adhesive and the cracked side can be turned toward the same side as the electrical cord in the fountain.

No matter how eager you are to get started, first read the owner's manual from front to back and do some practice drilling on an item similar to what you will be drilling for your fountain. Set your drill to its slowest setting. To decrease the chances of breakage, begin by drilling a pilot hole. (Pilot holes are made with the smallest bit you have in the center of the location you want your final hole.) Drill a second hole in the same location with a slightly larger bit, then repeat with a bit the size of the final hole you desire.

Support Systems

Not all fountain designs require support systems, but they're easy to create when needed. There are a variety of clever ways to add support to fountains.

When you'd like the water to spill out in a totally upright position or when you're building up a fountain with heavy materials such as rocks and your tubing is crimping, plastic piping can be a great help. Just cut a piece to the needed length and slip it over the tubing. If the piping will show in the finished fountain, consider adding decorative touches with craft paints. Copper piping and bamboo can be used in the same way, although they're usually more expensive.

Plastic piping is sometimes used to create an upright flow of water or to protect plastic tubing from unwanted crimping or bending. The piping can be embellished with acrylic paints if it will be seen in the finished fountain.

Cutting mouse holes for water flow and the electrical cord in terra cotta pots and underliners is a simple process with a multi-purpose drill bit.

A plastic plumbing coupling creates a flat surface to rest fountain materials upon. Be sure to make enough holes to provide a good water flow to the pump.

Many fountain designs require a flat surface for materials to rest upon or call for materials that are so heavy that their weight could damage the pump if they were placed directly on top of it. Plastic cups, terra cotta pots, and plumbing couplings make creative support structures in these types of fountains. This element will never be seen in your finished fountain, so looks are not important. Choose the easiest material to cut that will support the weight you plan to rest on it. In the fountain shown on page 72, for example, craft foam shapes needed a flat surface to rest on. Since they weigh very little, mouse holes were cut into a plastic drinking cup with great success and little effort. In the fountain on page 65, a terra cotta pot, which is visible in the finished fountain, was used for the same reason. (Terra cotta, by the way, cuts like butter with a multi-purpose drill bit.) For heavier materials, such as the sheets of slate rock in the fountain on page 40, a plastic coupling (available in plumbing departments in hardware stores) makes a great support system.

BASIC ASSEMBLY

Before you begin making a real fountain, it may help to spend some time re-inforcing the basic building ideas you learned on pages 22 to 24. Begin the process by browsing through the illustrations on pages 30–33 and through the finished fountains featured on pages 38–126. Avoid the temptation to read the how-to instructions. Instead, force yourself to mentally dissect the fountain: try to imagine where the pump is hidden, where the tubing has been placed, what holes had to be drilled to facilitate the tubing, etc. Then take a field trip to a store that sells finished fountains. The fountains can be small or large; it's the concept that counts. Look at a finished fountain and again mentally dissect the parts. Then peek under the concealers or inside the containers to test your assumptions.

The illustrations that follow will guide you through the building process of two types of fountains. As you're reviewing the illustrations, try to mentally substitute other types of materials and imagine how they might work in a fountain. Marbles or special stones could easily cover the pump instead of seashells for instance, or a handbuilt wooden box could be substituted for a ceramic bowl.

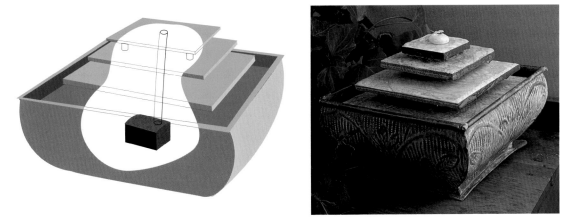

A well-done fountain dissuades the viewer from thinking about the mechanics. As a novice fountain maker, though, thinking about how the mechanics are assembled and hidden is an important part of the learning process.

Here are two of the simplest, most basic fountain designs. Most of the tabletop fountains in this book are either built with these techniques or with very clever variations. The seashell fountain at left uses a simple, build-around technique. To build a fountain like this one, first place your pump in the middle of the bowl/basin and insert a length of plastic tubing into the pump. Next, begin building interesting (and waterproof) materials around the pump and the tubing. The goal is to disguise the pump, create an eye-appealing design, and divert the water in an interesting flow. Large rocks (see the fountain on page 38) are also ideal for this type of fountain. Re-arranging the materials every few days to create different designs and water flows is a great way to learn the subtleties of fountain building.

This type of fountain construction is not a good idea when you're filling the bowl/basin with small, dense materials (such as small stones or marbles) that can easily block the water flow to the pump's intake filters. The fountain design at right uses a plastic plumbing coupling to protect the pump's intake filters and create a flat, sturdy surface for stacking or layering materials over. (See the fountains on pages 49 and 79 for examples.) The coupling is prepared with a series of grooves (a.k.a. "mouse holes") and/or slits that allow the coupling to sit over the pump without crimping the electrical cord as well as let a smooth flow of water in to the pump's intake filters.

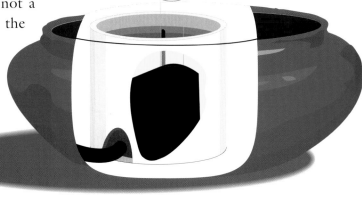

The key to dissecting this fountain is identifying the function of each element. The large, inverted pot on the right disguises the pump and tubing, while the smaller pots and saucers guide the water flow. The larger, upright pot is merely decoration.

The extreme simplicity of this fountain's design is disguised by special effects created with decorative paint. The pump and tubing hide under the inverted clay pot. A large mouse hole cut in the back side of the pot created space for the electrical cord and for water flow.

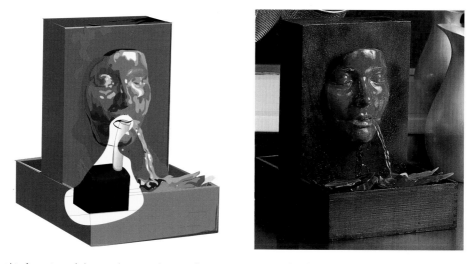

This fountain and the one shown at the top of page 33 are more similar than an untrained eye would think. A rectangular basin replaces the circular one, while a broader, wooden box replaces the taller, slate one to disguise the pump. The tubing is worked through the lips of the face instead of being trimmed flush with the top of the slate box.

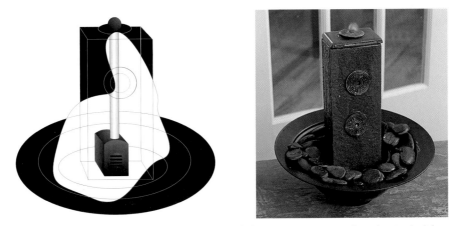

Imagine a long length of tubing standing upright in a small, black pump. Not a pretty sight, right? Simply slide a box over the pump, place the assembly in a basin of water, and—voila—a fountain is born.

A plumbing coupling prepared with mouse holes slides easily over a pump to create a flat surface onto which layers of slate can be stacked. Each piece of slate has a hole through its center. When the holes are aligned, it's easy to thread tubing through them, allowing the water to spill over the top and down over the layers of slate.

Although you may not see an initial resemblance between this fountain and the one in the center of page 32, their basic building design is virtually identical. A large bowl replaces the clay pot, while a large basin replaces the clay liner. The tubing is worked through the body and mouth of a decorative frog instead of being trimmed flush with the top of the pot.

DEALING WITH DETAILS

Once you've finished assembling a basic fountain as directed above, you may well believe that you're done. Ah, contraire. Assembling a fountain is the easy part. Now comes the challenging part, the part that can try your patience and challenge your creativity. It's time to futz. In fountain making, futzing involves the fine tuning of water flow to improve both sound and looks.

Water Acoustics

Until you plug in your first fountain, you may not be consciously aware of how many possible sounds water can make and how these sounds feel to you when you're living with them day in, day out. Do you want a gurgle? Do you want bubbling? Or perhaps you want to hear a rush of water movement. If you don't find your fountain's initial sound soothing, or if you just want to experiment with other possibilities, try adjusting the materials in your fountain so that the water moves differently. Rocks can be stacked or criss-crossed to create different sounds. Exchanging river pebbles for lava rocks can also alter the sound. Futzing with the sound may be a long-term process, with you exchanging rocks every time you pass by.

Water Flow

Futzing with the way the water looks can be a fun—and a wet—experience, so protect the area around your fountain with bath towels. For a gurgling, bubbly effect, try trimming the plastic tubing about ½ to 1 inch (13 to 25 mm) below the surface. For water pressure that's too strong, try placing a decorative bead or marble on top of the water flow.

Preventing Problems

Your mother was right: it's easier to prevent problems than to fix them, and fountains are no exception. A little attention to the issues presented here may well save you the hassle and expense of blown fuses, burned out pump motors, major messes, and worse.

Safety

Before plugging in your finished fountain, always doublecheck to make sure that the cord is not crimped or constricted by rocks or other materials. Sometimes cord crimps are just accidents, but often they are the direct result of crafters trying very hard to prevent the cord from showing in the finished fountain. If you find yourself tempted by a strong desire to hide the cord, give it up. It's not worth the safety risk or the risk of frustrating yourself into a completely unartistic state. Fountains use electricity to pump the water and electricity requires a cord: it's just that simple.

Another worthwhile precaution is to create a "drip loop" in the electrical cord. A well-crafted drip loop ensures that water dripping out of the fountain and down the electrical cord will fall to the floor, and not drip into the electrical socket. (See illustration.)

It's a good idea to always turn off your fountain (the same way you do your television and lights) before leaving the house for even short trips. Besides the obvious energy-saving benefits, fountains occasionally take in air and start spewing water. Left unattended, a spewing fountain can quickly lower the water levels enough to burn out the pump's motor, not to mention soak your furniture or carpet.

Water Levels

It pays to keep an occasional eye on the water level in your fountain, since water levels that are too low can cause the motor to burn out and possibly cause a fire. (The water level should always cover the pump's intake filters by at least an inch.) Evaporation levels depend on atmospheric moisture levels, and can vary from week to week and location to location. Thirsty pets can also contribute to low water levels. You might find it helpful to connect checking your fountain's water level with another regularly scheduled task such as watering the indoor plants or scrubbing the kitchen floor.

Maintenance

A noticeable decrease in your pump's performance is a good indication that it's time for a cleaning. Plant debris, dead insects, and other items can accumulate around your pump's motor and cause problems. Refer to the manufacturer's instructions that came with your pump for cleaning specifics. A small brush or a stream of water will usually be enough to remove any debris. Replacement filters are also available in many stores or by mail order from the manufacturer.

Mineral deposits from hard water can also cause performance problems. To remove hard water buildup, place your pump in a large plastic bowl, add a bottle of white vinegar, and run the pump for an hour or so. (Do not leave the pump in the vinegar for an extended period of time.) Rinse the pump and the bowl with water, then run the pump in plain water to clean.

If your fountain is difficult to disassemble, the vinegar can be added directly to your fountain as long as your fountain's materials won't react adversely with the vinegar. Test the materials by adding a few drops of vinegar. If you hear a buzzing sound and/or see small bubbles, then the vinegar is reacting and could possibly cause damage. Note: It's important to distinguish between vinegar reacting with a fountain material and vinegar reacting with some type of bacteria or mold that's on the surface of the materials. You can be sure it's the latter by scrubbing a small area and then adding a second drop of vinegar. If it doesn't bubble this time, then you can safely proceed with the vinegar treatment.

Unwelcome Guests

A host of microscopic life forms may welcome your fountain into your home with as much joy as you do. When present in limited numbers, algae, bacteria, and other small life forms can usually coexist in your fountain without causing problems. As their numbers increase, however, your irritation may also increase. Cleaning the water basin with bleach or a bleach substitute every few months may be necessary; just be sure to rinse the fountain well after cleaning. If small children or pets don't have access to your fountain, you might want to explore the many algicides available on the market. Look for them in aquarium departments and larger garden shops.

DESIGNERS:
Dawn Cusick
and
Celia Naranjo

Simple Rock Fountain

Here's a good example of how easy it can be to make a great fountain. All you need is a nice bowl, some interesting rocks and marbles, and the willingness to play around a little until you get the desired effect.

MATERIALS

- Bowl
- 4" (10 cm) plastic coupling
- Submersible pump
- Enough rocks and marbles to fill the bowl
  (Note: Only the top rocks will show in the finished fountain, so if the rocks you love are scarce or very expensive, consider using ordinary garden rocks or stones for the under layers.)

INSTRUCTIONS

1 Prepare the coupling as directed on page 28. Position the pump in the bottom center of the bowl and place the coupling over it with the largest opening over the electrical cord. Set the pump on its lowest pressure setting. Add enough water to cover the pump's intake filters.

2 Begin layering rocks around the coupling, leaving the area directly over the pump open for now. Scatter marbles between the rocks. Plug in the pump and note how the water is flowing. Add loose arrangements of rocks over the pump until you find a water flow and sound that you find pleasant.

39

Lotus Bowl Fountain

The classic beauty of this simple fountain can be changed as your whim dictates. Add a small cluster of air plants off to one side. Or change the bowl with the seasons.

MATERIALS

- Bowl or basin
- Submersible pump
- 4" (10 cm) plastic coupling
- Masonry bits and drill
- Small, decorative garden stones
- 4 pieces of slate, 3 approximately ½ the width of the bowl and 1 smaller piece
- Polyurethane

INSTRUCTIONS

1 Prepare the coupling as directed on page 28. Position the pump in the center of the bowl and place the coupling over the pump so that the electrical cord comes through the larger hole. Set the water pressure switch on its lowest setting. Fill the space around the coupling with stones.

2 Use a hammer and chisel to shape the larger slate pieces if desired. Ideally, each piece should be slightly smaller than the piece on which it rests. Play with different stacking positions and mark them roughly in the center. Drill a ½"(13 mm) hole through each of the three pieces.

3 Cover all four slate pieces with a coat of polyurethane. Allow to completely dry, then turn them over and do the other sides. Hot glue several small stones onto the back side of the smallest slate piece to serve as spacers. Carefully place the largest piece of slate on top of the pump's outtake opening, then add the remaining slate pieces, taking care to line up the holes. Add water to the bowl and plug in the pump. Increase the water pressure setting if necessary.

Slate Box Fountain

The tall slate box in this fountain serves to disguise the pump and the plastic tubing. The circular, rock-filled ring at the bottom of the fountain—a thrift store find that was once part of an outdoor grill—is not actually a working part of the fountain.

MATERIALS

- Slate tile
- Ceramic drill bits and drill
- Epoxy
- Silicone caulk
- Submersible pump
- Length of plastic tubing about 1" (2.5 cm) longer than the height of your box
- Bowl (an old salad bowl was used here)
- Circular ring, sanded and painted if necessary
- River stones
- Polyurethane
- Small accents or design elements to embellish the box (optional)

INSTRUCTIONS

1   Visit a tile store and find five pieces of slate tile to build a box. The box in this fountain was made from two pieces of slate measuring 12" x 4" (30 x 10 cm), two pieces measuring 12" x 2½" (30 x 6 cm), and one piece measuring 4" x 3" (10 x 7.5 cm). Ask the store to cut the tiles down to smaller sizes if necessary. (Note: Feel free to vary the box size as much as you like.)

2   Wearing protective eyewear, cut out a ¾" (18 mm) mouse hole at the bottom center of one of the 12" x 4" pieces. Drill a ½" hole in the center of the 4" x 3" piece. Epoxy the edges of the larger tile pieces together to form a box, sealing the seams with silicone as you add each side.

3   Position the pump in the center of the bowl and insert the tubing into the pump's adapter. Set the pump's water pressure to its lowest setting. Place the slate box over the pump, aligning the mouse hole over the pump's electrical cord. Insert the tubing through the top tile piece and move it down the tubing until it rests on the box.

4   Add enough water to the bowl to cover the pump's intake area. Plug in the pump to check the water pressure and adjust if necessary. Trim the plastic tubing flush with the tile. Add decorative accents to the box if desired.

5   Polyurethane one side of the stones and allow to completely dry. Place the ring over the box until it rests on the bowl. Fill the ring with stones. Sprinkle the stones with a few drops of water for a more realistic look.

Tile Fountain

A series of square tiles in descending sizes makes a handsome surface for water to fall over. For a slightly different look, turn the tiles on their diagonal or increase the spacing between tiles.

MATERIALS

- Decorative, square bowl
- 4 pieces of decorative tile (refer to text for sizes)
- Ceramic drill bits and drill
- Protective eyewear
- Submersible pump
- 10" (25 cm) length of plastic tubing
- 4" (10 cm) coupling
- 2 1" squares of ¼" thick plexiglass for spacers*
- 2 1" squares of ⅜" thick plexiglass for spacers*
- Decorative bead

*Note: It's not critical that the spacers be exactly these thicknesses; other thicknesses can be used, as can other materials, such as varnished wood or polymer clay.

INSTRUCTIONS

1 Bring your bowl to a tile store and look for square tiles that will complement both the bowl and the location you plan to display the finished fountain. Find four pieces of tile, one ½" (13 mm) smaller on all sides than the basin and the remaining three about 1" (2.5 cm) smaller on all sides than the tile it will rest on. If you find the perfect tile but it's the wrong size, just ask the store to cut it down. (Note: Purchasing two or three of each tile is an inexpensive safeguard against occasional drilling breakage.)

2 Prepare the coupling as described on page 28. Drill a ½" hole in each tile. Hire a glass shop to drill ½" holes in each spacer (it's worth the minimal charge) or cut spacers from wood and drill them or make the spacers from polymer clay and make a ½" hole with a pencil before baking.

3 Place the pump in the center of the basin and position the coupling over the pump so that the electrical cord comes out through the large hole. Set the pump on its lowest pressure setting. Insert the tubing into the pump's adapter.

4 Align the largest tile's hole over the tubing with its right side facing up and gently slide the tile down the tubing until it rests on the coupling. Slide one ¼" thick spacer and one ⅜" spacer down over the tubing until they rest on top of the tile. Gently slide the next largest tile over the tubing, right side facing up, until it rests flush with the spacers. Slide the remaining ⅜" spacer down the tubing. Add the next largest tile as you did the previous ones and slide the remaining ¼" spacer down the tubing. Slide the remaining tile down the tubing until it rests on the spacer.

5 Mark the tubing with an ink pen at the point where it's flush with the top tile. Remove the top tile and cut the tubing just below this mark. Add the tile back again and fill the bowl with water. Plug in your pump and place a decorative bead over the center hole. Voila!

Porch Fountain

Here's the perfect fountain to display on a porch or on a counter lined with house plants. The fountain rests on a verdigris planter that has been embellished with decorative garden ornaments.

MATERIALS

- Garden ornaments compatible with your plant stand
- Epoxy or other suitable adhesive
- Plant stand
- Glass bowl that securely fits in the plant stand
- Submersible pump
- 3" (7.5 cm) length of plastic tubing
- Several handfuls of interesting rocks

INSTRUCTIONS

1 Adhere the garden ornaments to the plant stand and allow them to completely dry. Place the glass bowl in the stand and position the pump in the bottom of the bowl. Set the water pressure at its lowest setting. Insert the tubing into the adapter.

2 Fill the area around the pump with rocks, taking care to disguise the tubing as well as possible. Add enough water to cover the rocks and plug in the pump. Add additional water or change the pressure setting on the pump if needed.

47

Circuit Board Fountain

An adventuresome spirit and a hand drill are all you need to create one-of-a-kind fountains from recycled materials. In this fountain, a stack of drilled and water-sealed circuit boards creates an interesting water flow surface.

MATERIALS

- 4" (10 cm) coupling
- Basin in roughly the same shape as the circuit boards
- Submersible pump
- Piece of slate just a little larger than a circuit board
- 5 circuit boards
- Metal and ceramic drill bits and drill
- Protective eyewear
- 8" (20 cm) length of plastic tubing
- Spacers (coins, stones, etc.)
- Glue gun and hot glue

INSTRUCTIONS

1 Prepare the coupling as described on page 28. Place the pump in the center of the basin, then place the coupling over the pump so that the mouse hole fits over the electrical cord. Set the pump to its lowest pressure setting.

2 Place the slate over the coupling and mark the spot where the tubing should come through with a crayon or chalk pencil. Drill a ½" (13 mm) hole through the marked spot. Repeat the step above with all five of the circuit boards.

3 Place the circuit boards on top of the slate and experiment with different thicknesses and positions of spacers until you find a look you like and one that enhances the falling effect of the water. (Note: The designer of this fountain used scrap computer parts for spacers and positioned them so that they show in the finished fountain.) Carefully thread the tubing through the circuit boards and slate. Insert the tubing into the pump's adaptor and work the slate down the tubing until it rests on the coupling. Gently work the circuit boards down the tubing.

4 Add water to the basin and plug in the pump. Adjust the water pressure if needed. If you're happy with the fountain, unplug the pump and hot-glue the spacers permanently in place. If you're not happy, experiment with different thicknesses of spacers and repeat the above steps. Trim the tubing so that it protrudes just a little over the top circuit board.

49

Picnic Basket Fountain

Although baskets aren't a common fountain-making material, when lined with an inexpensive plastic basin they're a great choice. The fountain can also be used as a vase: just drop fresh-cut flowers down into the water.

MATERIALS

- Picnic basket with top
- Plastic basin to fit inside basket
- Submersible pump
- Turquoise acrylic spray paint
- Varnish and brush
- Electrical tape and waterproof caulking
- ¼" (6 mm) bamboo sticks or wooden dowels
- Glue gun
- Slotted wood serving tray that fits inside basket
- Moss
- Interesting natural accent (a dried fungus was used here)

INSTRUCTIONS

1 Carefully work a hole just large enough for your fountain's electric plug in the center back side of the basin about 2" (5 cm) up from the bottom. Spray paint the basin and allow to completely dry, then finish with three coats of waterproofing varnish, allowing each coat to completely dry before adding the next.

2 After the last coat of varnish has completely dried, position the pump in the center of the basin and insert the plug through your opening. Carefully tape the gaps around the cord, then caulk the area to make it completely waterproof.

3 Experiment with the position of the tray to find a height that pleases you. Cut four pieces of bamboo or dowels to the necessary height, then glue one at each of the two lower bottom corners of the tray and one several inches in to the center from both of the top corners.

4 Hot glue a moss border around the basket and a few sprigs around the bamboo legs. Hot glue a dried flower or two and a large natural accent in one corner if desired.

51

Mermaid Fountain

Special design accents, such as the mermaid in this fountain, can be incorporated into a fountain with little effort. Using tacky wax or rubber caulking to secure the piece in place prevents damage and also allows you to easily substitute new items as your whim dictates.

MATERIALS

- Colorful bowl
- Submersible pump
- 4" (10 cm) coupling
- Slate pieces, one piece slightly larger than the opening of the bowl and several smaller pieces
- Masonry bits and drill
- Glue gun
- 6" (15 cm) length of plastic tubing
- Decorative accent

INSTRUCTIONS

1 Invert your bowl on top of the large slate piece and trace the bowl's outline in chalk or crayon. Using a hammer and chisel, carefully break off the edges to create a circular shape about ½ to 1" (13 to 25 mm) smaller than the bowl's opening.

2 Prepare the coupling as directed on page 28. Position the pump in the center of the bowl with a hole over the electrical cord. Set the pump's pressure switch on its lowest setting.

3 Begin playing with different stacking arrangements of smaller pieces of slate. After you've settled on an arrangement, drill ½" holes through all but the top piece of slate.

(The holes can be in the center of the pieces or off to one side; just be sure that the arrangement looks the way you intended when the holes are aligned on top of each other.)

4 Hot-glue your rock arrangement together, taking care to align the holes. Thread the tubing through the holes, leaving the excess protruding from the bottom rock. Decide where you want the rock arrangement to sit in your finished fountain and mark the spot on the large, circular piece of slate.

5 Drill a ½" hole in the large slate piece to line up with the rock arrangement. Thread the excess tubing through the circular rock and into the pump, repositioning the coupling and the pump if necessary to get the correct alignment.

6 Add water to the bowl and plug in the pump. Watch how the water flows for a few minutes to help you decide where to locate the accent element. Unplug the pump and allow the rock to completely dry, then attach your accent element. If you liked the way the water flowed, you're finished. For a more subtle flow of water, hot glue four small rocks to the bottom of a small piece of slate, then position this piece of slate face up over the hole.

DESIGNER:

Susan Kinney

Trinkets and Treasures Fountain

Tabletop fountains make a wonderful place to display natural collectibles such as shells, stones, beads, and other travel souvenirs. Don't be too quick to eliminate possibilities. Items that don't do well with frequent water contact, such as coins and other metals, can easily be coated with a protective coat of polyurethane.

MATERIALS

- Brass bowl or basin
- Submersible pump
- Several handfuls of stones, shells, etc

INSTRUCTIONS

1 Position the pump in the center back of your bowl or basin and adjust the pressure switch to its lowest setting. Choose a dozen of your favorite treasures and set them aside. Layer the remaining items loosely throughout the bowl and around the pump, taking care to leave breathing room around the pump's intake vents.

2 Fill the basin with water and plug in your pump. Adjust the water pressure setting if necessary. Leave the pump's outtake area uncovered for a drinking fountain water flow or loosely arrange treasures around the water outtake area for a more subtle water flow.

DESIGNER:

Jean Wall Penland

Marble Fountain

The rings of marble surrounding the pump and the water conduit were both created from discarded scraps (free!) from a stoneworks shop. The same design concept can easily be applied to other materials, making this a good fountain to showcase inexpensive collectibles.

MATERIALS

- 14" (36 cm) plastic plant underliner, with or without embossed patterns
- Acrylic spray paint
- Spray sealant
- Scraps of marble chunks
- Submersible pump
- Epoxy
- Masonry drill bits and drill (optional)
- Scrap of plastic cabinet material (Corian, for example) or a 6" (15 cm) length of ½" (13 mm) plastic piping

INSTRUCTIONS

1 Paint the underliner with two coats of spray paint and one coat of sealant, allowing each coat to completely dry before adding the next.

2 Position the pump in the middle of the underliner. Begin playing with different arrangements of stacked marble until you've created a ring around the pump that is deep enough to disguise the pump. If some of your pieces are too large to curve them around the pump, turn them upside down and hit them with a hammer until you get pieces of a workable size. Secure the marble pieces together with epoxy in small units, then arrange them again around the pump.

3 Create a decorative water conduit by trimming a piece of Corian to 1" square and 6" long. Drill a ½" hole through the center of the Corian, then polish the outside. Alternatively, spray paint a piece of plastic piping black. Align the Corian or the piping over the pump's adapter. Fill the underliner with enough water to make the pump run efficiently. Adjust the water pressure as needed.

Brass Fountain

An ordinary brass vase with a stand can be transformed into a fountain with little effort. A recycled lamp fixture makes the perfect conduit (the water travels through the space formerly used to carry electric wires), and creates a bubbly fountain flow reminiscent of champagne on ice.

MATERIALS

- Clean, empty can (old coffee cans work well)
- Metal drill bits and drill
- Protective eyewear
- Heavy gloves
- Submersible pump
- 14" (30 cm) length of plastic tubing
- Brass lamp fixture in a height that complements the vase (thrift stores are inexpensive sources)
- Electrical tape
- Brass vase with stand
- Two handfuls of rocks (they won't be visible in the finished fountain)

INSTRUCTIONS

1 Wearing gloves to prevent metal cuts, make a 1" (2.5 cm) mouse hole at the top of the can. Turn the can upside down and drill a ½" hole in the center top. Insert the tubing into the pump's adapter, then thread the tubing through the can and slide the can down over the pump so that the mouse hole is over the electrical cord.

2 Set your pump's water pressure to its lowest setting. Place the can-covered pump in the bottom of a mixing bowl filled with several inches of water. Slide the lamp fixture down over the tubing and plug in the pump. Adjust the pump's setting if needed. From this point on, you will have to disassemble the fountain in order to change the water pressure setting, so be sure you're happy with the water flow before moving on.

3 Remove the can-covered pump and the lamp fixture from the bowl and allow to completely dry. Slide the lamp fixture down over the tubing and secure the fixture tightly to the can with electrical tape. Place the pump assembly back into the mixing bowl and plug in the pump. Watch the taped area for leaks and retape if necessary. Remove the pump assembly from the mixing bowl.

4 Carefully lower the pump assembly down into the bottom of the vase. Fill the area around the can with rocks to increase stability. Trim off any excess plastic tubing just below the top of the lamp fixture. Add water to the vase and enjoy.

Shell Fountain

Assembling this small tabletop fountain reveals how simple it is to construct indoor fountains. Feel free to use the same concept— arranging attractive (and waterproof) objects creatively around a pump—to make any number of inventive fountains.

MATERIALS
- Submersible pump
- Small waterproof bowl or basin (this one was an inexpensive thrift store find)
- Spray acrylic paint in a color to match your bowl (optional)
- Interesting assortment of shells (large clam shells work especially well)
- 3" (7.5 cm) length of plastic tubing
- Epoxy

INSTRUCTIONS

1 Position the pump in the center back of your bowl. Since this is a fairly small fountain, you may find the prominence of the electrical cord to be distracting. If so, spray with several coats of paint, allowing the paint to completely dry between coats.

2 Insert the tubing into the pump and turn the pump to its lowest setting. Arrange the shells creatively around the pump and the tubing, working both to disguise the pump and to create an attractive arrangement. Add water and plug in.

3 Play with the arrangement of the shells if you're not happy with the sound and/or look of your fountain. Unplug the fountain, dry off the shells, and secure them in your chosen arrangement with epoxy.

61

DESIGNER:

Lee Davis

Natural Collage Fountain

Collections of interesting materials can be incorporated into a fountain with one-of-a-kind results. The fountain here combines several pieces of pottery, a piece of driftwood, and a candle into an interesting fountain. If you have trouble finding the materials to make this fountain, consider visiting a ceramic studio and asking for scraps.

MATERIALS

- Large bowl
- Submersible pump
- 10" (25 cm) length of plastic tubing
- Masonry bits and drill
- Protective eyewear
- Flat rock about half the size of the bowl's width
- Piece of flat pottery a little smaller than the above rock (another flat rock can be substituted)
- 4–5" (10-12.5 cm) ceramic bowl
- Driftwood
- Flat piece of pottery approximately 8" (20 cm) long (a second piece of driftwood can be substituted)
- Several pieces of fired pottery shapes in assorted sizes
- Several small stones
- Candle in ceramic holder
- Several interesting leaves

INSTRUCTIONS

1 Place the pump in the center of the bowl and adjust its water pressure to the lowest setting. Hold the large rock over the pump and decide how you'd like it to be positioned. (Move the pump if necessary.) Use a crayon or chalk pencil to mark the spot where the tubing will come through. Repeat with the largest pottery piece and the small bowl. Drill ½" (13 mm) holes through the marked locations.

2 Thread the tubing through all three pieces, then insert the tubing into the pump and carefully lower the large rock down until it rests on the pump. Create small "shelves" in the fountain by placing the driftwood and the 8" piece of pottery at angles along the edges of the bowl as shown in the photo.

3 Arrange the remaining pieces of pottery and the candle around the fountain, using the photo as a guide. Fill the bowl with water and plug in the pump. Unplug the pump. Adjust the water pressure if necessary and trim the plastic tubing to ½" above the bowl. Plug the pump back in. Place the small rocks in the ceramic bowl and play with their positioning to adjust the fountain's water flow and sound. Add several fresh-cut leaves to the water. Replace the leaves periodically to prevent them from decaying in the water and clogging the pump's filters.

Terra Cotta Patio Fountain

The incredible simplicity of this fountain's design will leave you amazed.
The flat surface created by the inverted underliner is ideal for potted plants
or anything else you'd like to display.

MATERIALS

- Polyurethane and brush
- 14" (36 cm) clay underliner
- 7" (17 cm) clay underliner
- 2 5" (12.5 cm) clay underliners
- 2½" (6 cm) clay underliner
- 6" (15 cm) clay pot
- 4" (10 cm) clay pot
- 2" (5 cm) clay pot
- Clay drill bits and drill
- Protective eyewear
- Submersible pump
- 6" length of plastic tubing
- River rocks
- Potted plant, optional
- Small statue, optional

INSTRUCTIONS

Apply three coats of polyurethane to all of the underliners and pots, allowing each coat to completely dry before adding the next. Prepare the 3", the
7", and one of the 5" underliners by cutting ¾" (18 mm) mouse holes in
them. Cut four mouse holes at opposite sides to each other in the remaining
5" underliner. Cut a mouse hole at the top of the 6" pot. Drill a ½" (13 mm)
hole in the bottom center of the 7" underliner. Insert the plastic tubing into
the pump.

2 Begin assembling the fountain by placing the pump at one edge of the 14" underliner. Set the pump to its lowest setting. Invert the 6" pot over the pump with the electrical cord extending out of the mouse hole and the tubing coming out of the center hole. Thread the tubing through the 7" underliner and lower it down until it rests on top of the pot.

3 Invert the 4" pot to the right of the large pot, then invert the 2" pot and place it toward the right front of the 4" pot. Place the 5" underliner on top of the 4" pot and the 2½" underliner on top of the 2" pot.

4 Fill the 14" underliner to its rim with water, making sure the water level covers the pump's intake filters. Plug in the pump. As the water begin spilling out of the larger pot, adjust the 7" underliner so that the water spills out of the mouse hole and down into the 5" underliner of the next pot. Repeat with the 5" underliner so that the water spills down into the 2½" underliner. Adjust the 2½" underliner so that the water spills down into the front of the 14" underliner. Reposition the pots as needed to achieve the best water flow.

5 Add river rocks to the 14" underliner. Add a few additional rocks to the smaller underliners as accents. A potted plant and/or a small statue can also be added.

Apple Java Fountain

Designing your own creative fountain is a simple challenge as long as you keep an open mind about potential materials. Any container that's large enough to disguise a submersible pump is fair game, as this coffee cup basin aptly demonstrates.

MATERIALS
- Oversized ceramic cup and saucer
- 1" (2.5 cm) length of plastic tubing
- Submersible pump
- Handful of interesting rocks or stones
- Ceramic drill bits and drill
- Ceramic* apple
  (*Apples made from other materials can be substituted if they are waterproof.)

INSTRUCTIONS
Insert the tubing into the pump's adapter and place the pump in the bottom of the cup. Set the pump on its lowest setting and loosely surround it with stones. Drill a ⅜" (9 mm) hole through the apple. Insert the tubing into the apple. Add water and enjoy.

DESIGNER:
Suzanne McCall

Simple Marble Fountain

Here's a versatile fountain design that can be adapted with the seasons by simply changing the bowl or the marbles. Small glass tree ornaments, for example, would look great in a gold bowl during the winter holiday season. A submersible light positioned near the pump adds playful highlights to the water and the marbles.

MATERIALS
- Large glass bowl
- Submersible pump
- Submersible light
- 3" (7.5 cm) of plastic tubing
- Marbles

INSTRUCTIONS

1   Position the pump and light unit on the bottom of the bowl. Insert the plastic tubing into the pump and set the pump on its lowest pressure setting.

2   Arrange the marbles in the bowl to disguise the pump. Fill the bowl with at least enough water to cover the pump's intake filters and plug in the pump and the light. Trim the plastic tubing if necessary and make any needed adjustments in water pressure, water levels, or pump placement.

DESIGNERS:
Dawn Cusick
and
Susan Kieffer

Oblong Brass Fountain

This simple-to-make fountain uses an oblong brass bowl and a small brass vase—both antique store finds—to create an interesting variation of the basic table-top bowl fountain.

MATERIALS

- Submersible pump
- Oblong brass bowl
- Hardware cloth
- Wire cutters
- Metal bits and drill
- Protective eyewear
- Small brass vase
- 10" length (25 cm) of plastic tubing
- River rocks

INSTRUCTIONS

1 Set the pump on its lowest pressure setting and position it at one end of the brass bowl. Measure the remaining length in the bowl and cut a piece of hardware cloth that's this length and three times the width. Fold the long edges of the hardware cloth over each other in thirds, then place it in the bowl.

2 Drill a ½" (13 mm) hole in the bottom of the vase. Place the vase on its side in front of the pump. Thread the tubing through the bottom of the vase and insert the other end into the pump. Experiment with different heights and angles for the vase, using rocks to prop it up.

3 Cover the hardware cloth, the area around the cord, and any remaining gaps with river rocks. Add enough water to the bowl to cover the pump's intake filters by more than an inch and plug in the pump. Make any desired adjustments in water pressure.

DESIGNERS:

Dawn Cusick

and

Celia Naranjo

Gift Package Fountain

Add a new twist to your holiday decorating with a fountain made from faux gift packages. Use the same concept to create fountains for wedding and birthday celebrations.

MATERIALS

- Large sheet of 2" thick (5 cm) craft foam
- Serrated knife
- Container (a rectangular glass baking dish was used here)
- 3 colors of foil or cellophane gift wrap
- Craft knife
- Scissors
- Disposable plastic cup
- Submersible pump
- 15" (37 cm) plastic tubing
- Decorative ribbon and bow set
- Handful of sewing pins
- Gift box just a little larger than your container

INSTRUCTIONS

1 Cut out a piece of foam that measures about 1" (2.5 cm) smaller on all edges than your container. Cut out a second piece of foam about 1½" (4 cm) smaller than the first piece on all edges. Cut a third piece of foam to the shape of a small package. Stack the three pieces of foam on top of each other (working from largest to smallest). If you're unhappy with the staggered sizing, trim additional foam off the middle and/or top pieces.

2 Mark the middles of all three pieces of foam with a marker or crayon on both sides. Using a pencil or other pointed object, make holes through the foam, making sure you go in at the middle mark and come back out at the middle mark on the other side. Neatly wrap all three pieces of foam as you would an ordinary gift. Find the center holes by pressing gently on the wrapped foam blocks, then use a craft knife to carefully cut out the paper over the holes. (Note: The holes won't be visible in the finished fountain, so don't obsess about imperfect cuts.)

3 Place the cup upside down next to your container and mark the container's height on the cup with a marker or crayon. Use scissors to trim the cup to ½" (13 mm) below the marked line. Prepare the cup the same way you would a coupling but using scissors instead of a drill. (Refer to page 28 if necessary.) Place the pump in the center of your container, then place the cup over it with the largest hole over the electrical cord. Set the pump to it's lowest water pressing setting.

73

4 Fill the container with water until the pump's intake filters are completely covered. Thread the plastic tubing through the holes in the wrapped packages, beginning with the largest package and finishing with the smallest. Insert the tubing into the pump's outake area, then gently work the packages down the tubing until the bottom one rests on top of the pump.

5 Arrange the ribbon around the packages, beginning at the center top with the ribbon just positioned behind the tubing and continuing down the sides. Secure the ribbon in place by inserting the sewing pins into the foam at an angle. Curve the plastic tubing away from the ribbon and plug in the fountain. Play with positioning the bow so that it appears that the water is coming out of the bow's center loop. Pin the bow in place, then unplug the fountain and trim off any excess tubing.

6 Place your container into a gift box and add gift tissue if desired. When the celebration's over, remove the plastic tubing from the pump's outake area. (The packages will come off with the tubing.) Pack up the packages with your other holiday decorations, then make a new fountain with the pump.

Mosaic Fountain

This small fountain looks great on a windowsill with a group of potted plants. Ceramic chips sold in craft stores for mosaic crafters make a nice alternative to rocks and marbles for disguising the pump.

MATERIALS
- Small mosaic bowl
- Submersible pump
- Mosaic chips
- Several large stones

INSTRUCTIONS

1 Set the pump on its lowest pressure and place it in the center of the bowl and setting. Place several large stones loosely around the pump, taking care not to block the area around the pump's intake filters.

2 Look through the mosaic chips and place about a dozen of your favorites aside. Fill the area around the stones and the pump with mosaic chips. Arrange your favorite chips on top. Fill the bowl with enough water to cover the pump's intake filters by more than an inch. Plug in the pump and make any necessary adjustments in water pressure. Note: If the water pressure is too high even on the pump's lowest setting, reduce the stream to a gurgle by arranging several large chips over the outtake hole.

DESIGNER:

Susan Kinney

Face Mask Fountain

Here's a contemporary alternative to the traditional, urinating-little-boy fountains. Although purchased masks work perfectly well, you may prefer to customize your fountain by making a face mask of your own or a loved one's face with a commercial molding product.

MATERIALS

- Wooden box with lid, approximately 7 x 10.5 x 3" high (17 x 26 x 7 cm)*
- Wooden box without lid, approximately 8 x 11 x 3" high (20 x 27 x 7 cm)*
- Wood water block/seal liquid
- Purchased or handmade mask with open mouth
- Submersible pump
- 10" (25 cm) length of plastic tubing
- Spray paint or lacquer
- Waterproof adhesive
- Aquarium sealant
- Tumbled glass shards (available in craft supply stores)

*Note: These sizes can vary as long as the lidded box fits neatly into the base box.

INSTRUCTIONS

1 Place the lidded box upright on its narrow side inside of the larger box. Drill a hole in the bottom corner of the lidded box at the height where the electrical cord of the pump will emerge. Make sure the hole is large enough for the plug to fit through.

2 Hold your mask against the upright box and experiment with different heights until you find a pleasing location. Mark the area where the mouth will be with a crayon or chalk pencil. Drill a ½" (13 mm) hole at the marked area.

3 Fill a large container with water sealant and soak the top and lid of the boxes for the length of time suggested by the manufacturer. If your mask is a purchased, wooden one, soak it at the same time. Allow the boxes to completely dry. Seal the inner bottom joints and corners with aquarium sealant and allow to completely dry. Paint or spray the boxes.

4 Place the pump in the lidded box and work the plug through the base hole. Insert the plastic tubing into the pump and then through the mask's mouth hole. Test the water pressure by placing the box and pump in a sink partially filled with water. Plug in the pump and adjust the water flow if necessary. Seal the lid closed (pump inside) with aquarium sealant.

5 Attach the mask to the outside of the upright box with a thin bead of aquarium sealant. Place the lidded, masked box in the larger box. Arrange the glass pieces in the base of the box and fill with enough water to cover the pump's intake filters by more than an inch (2.5 cm).

Pyramid Fountain

This fountain illustrates the virtually limitless possibilities of materials. The fountain's pyramid shape was made from a mold created with children's building blocks.

MATERIALS

- Interlocking building blocks
- Latex rubber
- Small, inexpensive paint brush
- Clear resin
- Glass drill bit and drill
- 4" (10 cm) coupling
- Submersible pump
- Glass bowl
- 10" (25 cm) length of plastic tubing
- Marbles or glass stones in a complementary color

INSTRUCTIONS

1   Build a pyramid with a base about an inch (2.5 cm) smaller than the opening of your bowl. Working on a flat, protected surface, paint a coat of latex rubber over the pyramid. Apply nine more coats of latex, allowing each coat to completely dry (usually takes 24 hours) before adding the next. Clean the brush in between coats as directed on the product label. After the last coat has completely dried, peel the rubber form off the pyramid.

2   Turn the rubber form mold upside down on a protected surface and brace it in a box or large mixing bowl with towels packed around it. Prepare the resin as directed on the product label, then pour it into the mold. After the resin has completely dried, remove the mold. Measure and mark the center of the pyramid's bottom surface and drill a hole up through the pyramid and out the top.

3   Prepare the coupling as shown on page 28. Place the pump in the center of the bowl, then place the coupling over it with a mouse hole over the cord. Set the pump's water pressure setting on its lowest setting and insert the tubing into the pump. Loosely fill the area between the coupling and the interior wall of the bowl with marbles or stones.

4   Thread the tubing through the pyramid until the pyramid's base rests on the coupling. Add water to the bowl and make sure that the pump's intake filters are receiving a good water supply. Plug in the pump, trim off any excess tubing, and make any necessary water flow adjustments. (Note: If the water comes out with too much force and your pump is on its lowest setting, you can add a marble or a bead to the water flow to slow it down. Another option is to remove the tubing and place the pyramid's hole directly over the pump's hole.)

Frog Fountain

Standing fountains make a versatile alternative to tabletop fountains. They can easily be made from purchased plant stands or from thrift store finds.

MATERIALS

- Plant stand with pot
- Spray water sealant
- Drill bits and drill
- Slightly smaller* pot in a matching or complementary color
- Accent ornament (the frog in this fountain came from a garden shop)
- Submersible pump
- 10" length (25 cm) of plastic tubing
- Decorator moss
- Handful of stones for accents

(*This pot needs to be small enough to fit inside the larger pot when turned upside down.)

INSTRUCTIONS

1 Prepare the larger pot by sealing any holes, painting if necessary, and spraying with two coats of water sealant. Prepare the smaller pot, if necessary, by drilling a ½" hole in the bottom center. Prepare the accent ornament, if necessary, by drilling a ½" hole through its bottom.

2 Position the pump in the middle of the larger pot. Insert the tubing into the pump and adjust the pump to its lowest setting. Turn the smaller pot upside down in the middle of the larger pot. If your smaller pot sits flush against the bottom of the larger pot, cut several ¾" (19 mm) mouse holes around the edges of the smaller pot to allow for water circulation. (If your smaller pot rests securely on the sides of the larger pot, creating at least a ¾" gap, then you won't have a problem with water circulation and can skip this step.)

3 Align one of the mouse holes (if you have one) over the cord and insert the tubing through the smaller pot's hole. Work the tubing through the bottom of the frog until it comes out of its mouth. Fill the larger pot with enough water to cover the pump. Plug in the pump and adjust the tubing, the direction of the frog, and the pump's setting as needed to create an attractive water flow. Arrange moss around the space separating the two pots. Add decorative stones and accents as desired. (Note: The rings in this fountain were originally part of the plant stand.)

Countertop Fountain

Here's an opportunity to create a fountain with colors and patterns customized to your home. Once you finish the decorating process, the fountain itself can be assembled in minutes.

MATERIALS

- Drill and masonry bits
- Protective eyewear
- 14" (36 cm) clay underliner
- 6" (15 cm) clay pot
- Artist's gesso
- Tube or bottle of titanium white acrylic paint
- Soft, wide brush
- Artist's varnish
- Cotton cloth or paper towels
- Bottle of blue fabric paint
- Ethyl alcohol
- Submersible pump
- 4" (10 cm) length of plastic tubing
- Bag of colorful marbles

INSTRUCTIONS

1 Prepare the clay pot as directed on page 28. Paint the clay underliner and the bowl (inverted) with one or two coats of artist's gesso and one or two coats of white acrylic paint, allowing each coat to completely dry before applying the next.

2 Brush a coat of blue fabric paint onto the rim or another selected area of your pot.

While the paint is still wet, wipe and rub off most of the paint with a cotton cloth or paper towel so that a stain remains. If the paint is too thick in some areas, use an ethyl alcohol–dampened cloth to carefully thin it out. After the paint dries, dip the end of the brush handle into the paint and touch it to the pot to create dots. After the pot has completely dried, finish with a coat of varnish on the pot and the underliner. (Note: If you have problems with blue paint encroaching where it shouldn't, carefully overpaint with titanium white before varnishing.)

3 Insert the plastic tubing into the pump's adapter and place the pump in the middle of the underliner. Set the pump's water pressure to its lowest setting. Position the inverted pot over the pump so that the cord protrudes out from the mouse hole and the plastic tubing comes out through the opening in the center of the pot. Trim the tubing flush with the pot. Fill the open area with a layer or two of marbles. Add water, taking care to make sure the water level is high enough for the pump to run efficiently. Adjust the pump's pressure if needed.

83

Stone Tower Fountain

Here's another eye-stopping fountain made from recycled materials. (The marble slab was once an old road marker.) Don't be intimidated about pouring your own cement bowl. Although you can always substitute a purchased bowl, this one is easy to make and is very lightweight.

MATERIALS

- Circular object for basin mold (an old, half-circle glass lamp shade was used here)
- Large plastic trash bag
- Plastic ball a little smaller than your mold (a basketball was used here)
- Small bag of portland cement mix
- Small bag of vermiculite soil additive (available in garden supply shops)
- Small bag of perlite soil additive (available in garden supply shops)
- 3' tall x 5" wide x 3" thick (.9 m x 12 cm x 7 cm) piece of carvable marble (Georgia marble is a good choice)
- Mason or grinding bits and drill
- Protective eyewear
- Chisels in several different sizes
- Paint scraper
- Concrete water sealant
- Submersible pump
- 3' (.9 m) length of plastic tubing
- Heavy tape
- Several handfuls of lightweight stones (lava rocks were used here)

INSTRUCTIONS

1 Line the inside of your mold with the plastic trash bag. Don't worry about folds and wrinkles in the bag—they will add an interesting texture to the outside of your bowl. Mix two parts portland cement to one part vermiculite and one part perlite. Stir the dry ingredients together, then begin slowly adding water and stirring until you get a syrup-like consistency.

2 Pour the cement mixture into the mold until the mold is half full. Place the basketball directly in the middle of the cement so that it floats about 2" (5 cm) away from the bottom and the sides of the mold. Stabilize the ball with some heavy objects (bricks were used here) and allow the cement to dry for at least 12 hours.

3 Turn the mold upside down, lift the basin off, and remove the garbage bag. Smooth off any uneven spots on your basin with a paint scraper. Allow the basin to sit for 24 hours, then treat with several coats of water sealant. After the sealant has completely dried, add water to the bowl and test for waterproofness; retreat with sealant if necessary.

4 Clean and sand the marble slab if necessary. Working on the back side of the marble, drill a hole with the ¼" bit in the center about 3" (7 cm) down from the top. Angle the drill as you work to create a 45-degree angle. Create several water pockets below the hole using grinding bits. Smooth the surface in each water pocket with the chisels.

5 Place the marble tower in the center front of the bowl and add stability by placing rocks around the marble base. Place the pump behind the marble and insert the tubing into the pump. Insert the other end of the tubing into the drilled hole so that the tubing comes out on the marble's front side. Secure the tubing to the back of the marble in several places with a small piece of heavy tape.

6 Set the pump's water pressure to its lowest setting. Add enough water to the bowl to cover the pump's intake filters by more than an inch. Plug in the pump and watch the water flow. Increase the pump's pressure setting if desired. Unplug the pump and trim the plastic tubing so that it rests just inside the drilled hole.

Water Spray Fountain

Creating novel water flows in a tabletop fountain is incredibly easy with the right tools. In the fountain shown here, a t-flow adapter fits easily into the plastic tubing. If you have trouble finding fountain accessories, visit the aquarium section of a large pet store.

MATERIALS
- Silver bowl
- Submersible pump
- 10" length of plastic tubing (25 cm)
- T-flow adapter
- Black marbles
- Clear glass pebbles

INSTRUCTIONS

1 Set the pump on its lowest pressure setting and place it in the middle of the bowl. Insert the plastic tubing into the pump and insert the t-flow adapter into the tubing. Hold the tubing upright to make sure it won't be more than an inch taller than your bowl. Remove the t-flow adapter and trim off any excess tubing.

2 Loosely fill the area around the pump with marbles and glass stones. Add water to the bowl. Plug in the pump and check the water flow. Adjust the water pressure setting if necessary. Disguise the top of the tubing with clear glass stones.

Stacked Squares Fountain

*Identical bowls in varying sizes can be used to make interesting, tiered foun-
tains. A layer of rolled-up hardware cloth inserted in the open space in the larger
bowl allows water to flow back down to the pump and also avoids the need to fill
up the entire bowl with glass pebbles.*

MATERIALS

- Matching square bowls, one about half the size of the other
- Coupling
- Submersible pump
- Drill and ceramic bits
- Protective eyewear
- 8" (20 cm) length of plastic tubing
- Square foot (.3 m) of hardware cloth
- Wire cutters
- Glass pebbles

INSTRUCTIONS

1   Prepare the coupling as directed on page 28. Place the pump in the center of the larger bowl and place the coupling over it so that the larger hole is over the electrical cord.

2   Drill a ½" (13 mm) hole in the bottom center of the smaller bowl. Place one end of the plastic tubing into the pump and thread the other end through the hole in the smaller bowl. Lower the bowl until it rests flat on the coupling. Set the pump on its lowest pressure setting.

3   Measure the length of two facing edges in the larger bowl's interior and cut two pieces of hardware cloth into squares that are this measurement. Roll the squares up and work them into the gaps on facing sides. Measure the distance of the two remaining sides of the bowl. Cut squares to fit and work them into the gap as you did the other two squares. Cut away a small amount of the hardware cloth to prevent the electrical cord from being crimped.

4   Trim the plastic tubing to ½" below the top of the bowl. Fill the top bowl with glass pebbles, taking care to place a large stone over the tubing if you'd like a gentle water flow. Cover the hardware cloth with glass pebbles. Plug in the pump and adjust the water flow if desired by rearranging the stones.

Gurgling Egg Fountain

A stroll through the aisles of your local garden shop may well inspire several fountains. The decorative planter, ceramic egg, and river rocks in this fountain were all garden supply store finds.

MATERIALS

- Ceramic planter and liner
- Submersible pump
- Coupling
- Hollow ceramic egg (this one was found in a garden shop)
- Drill and ceramic bits
- Protective eyewear
- 8" (20 cm) length of plastic tubing
- Square foot (.3 m) of hardware cloth
- Wire cutters
- River stones

INSTRUCTIONS

1   Prepare the coupling as directed on page 28. Place the liner inside the pot and the pump in the center of the liner. Place the coupling over the pump so that the mouse hole is over the electrical cord. Drill ½" (13 mm) holes through the center of the ceramic egg.

2   Thread the plastic tubing through the ceramic egg and the insert the tubing into the pump. Gently lower the egg down the tubing until it rests on the coupling. Set the pump on its lowest pressure setting.

3   Cut two pieces of hardware cloth into squares that are the length of your bowl's interior. Roll up the squares up and work them into the gaps on facing sides, creating as much of a flat surface as possible. Measure the distance of the two remaining sides of the bowl. Cut squares to this length and work them into the gap as you did the other two squares. Cut away a small amount of hardware cloth to prevent the electrical cord from being crimped.

4   Plug in the pump and adjust the water pressure if necessary. Unplug the pump and cover the wire surfaces with river rocks.

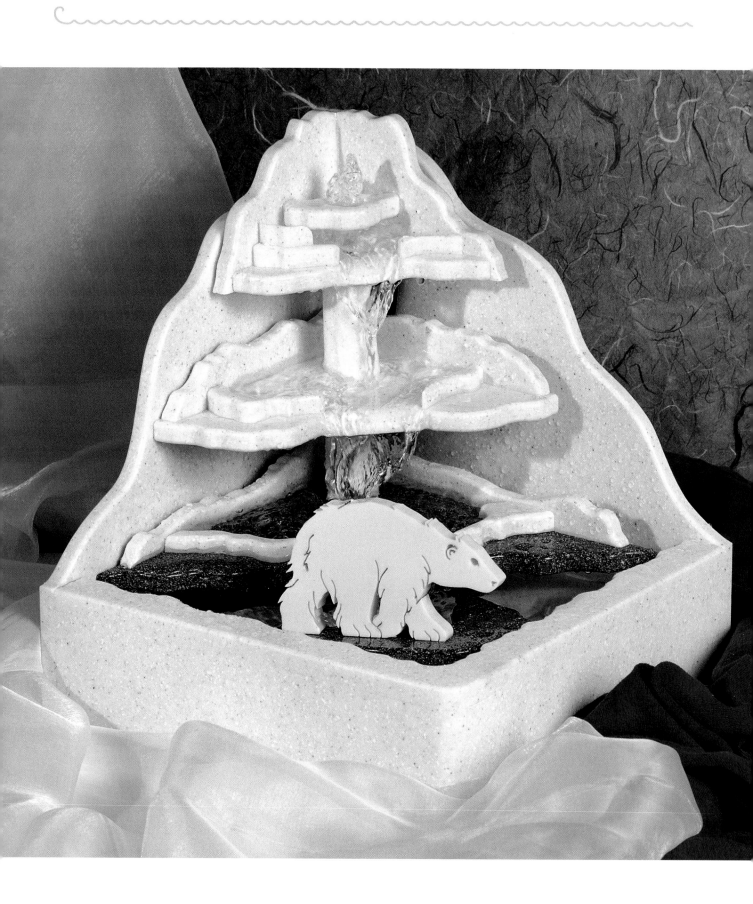

Cascading Corian Fountain

Although this fountain looks great made from Corian, the popular kitchen countertop material, it can also be made from plywood or standard dimension lumber. Just add some plastic tubing and epoxy cement (for waterproofing) to the materials list.

MATERIALS
- 24" x 30" (60 x 75 cm) piece of ½" (13 mm) thick white Corian
- 11½" square of ½" thick dark blue Corian (for base)
- Fine grit sandpaper
- Epoxy cement

TOOLS
- Table saw
- Band saw
- Drill with ceramic bits
- Protective eyewear

CUT LIST
- 1 back (L)   12" square (30 cm)
- 1 back   12" x 11½"
- 1 pool edge   2" x 11" (5 x 27 cm)
- 1 pool edge (L)   2" x 11½"
- 1 pool lip   2" x 9½" (5 x 23.5 cm)
- 1 pool lip (L)   2" x 1½" (5 x 4 cm)
- 2 bottom supports   2" x 1¼" (5 x 3 cm)
- 4 tier supports   1" x 2¾" (2.5 x 7 cm)
- 4 tier backs   1¼" x 8½" (3 x 21 cm), 1¼" x 8" (3 x 20 cm), 1¼" x 7" (3 x 17 cm), 1¼" x 6½ (3 x 16 cm)
- 1 top tier back   3" x 5½" (7.5 x 13.5 cm)
- 1 top floor   5" square (12 x 12 cm)
- 1 polar bear (see pattern on page 95)

93

INSTRUCTIONS

1 Cut out the Corian as directed in the cut list with a table saw. Sand all cut surfaces smooth to increase gluing adhesion. Round over all exposed corners.

2 Mark a point 3" up from the corner on back piece (L). Connect that point to the diagonally opposite corner. With this line as a reference, draw a curving line in pencil just above it and cut along this line with the band saw to form the back edge. (Save the scrap for floor 1.) Match the square edge of this piece to the other back and use the curved line as a pattern. Cut this side. (Save the scrap for floor 2 [base].)

3 Apply epoxy to two edges of the base. Line up back (L) with the front edge of the base. (The back edge will extend by ½".) Apply cement to the long edge of the other back and secure it with this assembly. It should now be even at all corners.

4 Apply epoxy to one short edge and one long edge of the pool edge. Position this along the front of the base from the back toward the front corner. Repeat with the pool edge (L). These steps form the pool.

5 Lay the two pool lip pieces flat with the shorter one butting into (L) to form a corner. Draw a wavy line in pencil along the inside length of these two pieces and cut out on the band saw. Position these pieces on the top of the pool edge so the curved side faces in, then cement in position.

6 On the scrap saved for floor 1, mark a point about 8¾" (22 cm) along each edge from the corner. Draw a line connecting these points. Find the center of this line and draw a line from that point to the corner. From the corner measure 1½" (4 cm) and drill a ½" hole. From the corner measure 6" (15 cm); measure 2" to either side of this point, then connect with a line parallel to the other long line. This space will form the waterfall area. Connect each end of the waterfall area to the 8¾" marks with curving lines and cut these with the band saw.

7 On the scrap saved for floor 2, repeat the above step, making the long edges 7¼" (18 cm), the distance from the corner 4¾"(11 cm), and the waterfall 3" wide. Make the top floor the same with a 5" edge and the waterfall 3" (7.5 cm) from the corner and 2" wide. The hole position is the same on both of these pieces.

8 Place the fountain pump in the back corner of the pool. Drill two ½" holes next to each other about 3" from the corner about 3" from the base. Be sure the hole is large enough to allow the electrical cord to exit the back. Position floor 1 above the pump. Mark the floor where the cord will go and then band saw a channel for it.

9 Cut a curved line along the tier backs, stepping it down as it approaches the front edges. Cement the 8½" and 8" tier backs to floor 1, and the 7" and 6½" backs to floor 2. They should be even with the back corner and resting upon the floor.

10 Cement the two bottom supports to the pool base positioned so they will uniformly support floor 1 yet not interfere with the pump. Apply cement to the back of the tier backs, the floor assembly, and the top of the supports; place in position. There should be a gap from each edge to the pool lip.

11 Cement the tier supports together to form 1" x 1" x 2¾" blocks. Drill a centered ½" hole the length of each block. Cement one onto floor 1, making sure the holes align and are clear of cement.

12 Apply cement to the back of the floor 2 assembly and the top of the tier support. Place this assembly snuggly against the back. Cement the next tier support, taking care to align the holes.

13 On the top tier back, mark a point ½" from one corner along the long edge; draw a line from that point to the opposite corner. Draw a curving line over this area, then cut it with the band saw. Cement these two back pieces together and to the floor. (The floor butts into these backs rather than upon them.) Cement this assembly to the pool back the same way as you did the previous floors.

14 Fashion a triangle from a piece of scrap with two sides of about 2" and the long edge a wavy line. Drill a ⅞" hole centered in it. Cement this piece about 1½" up on the top tier back.

15 Fashion curving pieces from scrap in any desired shape that will rest against the tier backs and reach just to the point of the waterfall straight edges. These shapes will form small pools at each level. Cement them in position.

Wading Flamingos Fountain

The lightweight, marble-like appeal of Corian makes it a great material for crafting fountains. Look for Corian wherever home building supplies are sold; for a smaller project such as this one, though, you may prefer to find a custom countertop maker and ask to purchase his/her scraps.

MATERIALS

- 12" x 15" (30 x 39 cm) Corian, ½" (13 mm) thick
- 12" (30 cm) square of Corian, ¼" (6 mm) thick in a second color
- 7" x 4¼" (17 x 10 cm) scrap piece of ½" thick Corian in a third color
- Epoxy cement
- Submersible pump
- 12" (30 cm) length of heavy-gauge jewelry wire

TOOLS

- Table saw
- Band saw/scroll saw
- Drill with ceramic bits
- Protective eyewear
- Fine grit sandpaper
- Wire cutters

CUT LIST FROM ½" CORIAN

- 1 base   7 x 8¾" (17 x 22 cm)
- 2 mid tiers   7 x 4½" (17 x 11 cm)
- 2 top tiers   5 x 3" (12 x 7 cm)
- 4 vertical supports 2 x 2⅜" (5 x 6 cm)
- 1 spout   1 x 2¼" (2.5 x 5 cm), cut from scrap

CUT LIST FROM ¼" CORIAN (12" SQUARE)

- 2 short walls   6½ x 2" (16 x 5 cm)
- 2 long walls   8¾ x 2" (22 x 5 cm)
- 1 corner support   2 x ⅜" (5 x .9 cm)

CUT LIST FROM ¼" CORIAN (7" X 4¼")

Trace and cut out two flamingos from the pattern on page 99.

INSTRUCTIONS

1 Cut out the Corian with a table saw as directed in the cut lists. Sand and smooth all cut surfaces to aid in adhesion. Round over corners and edges as desired.

2 On one mid tier piece, mark a spot 2¼" in from one long edge and 1¾" in from the short edge. Drill a ½" hole at the marked spot. On one top tier piece, mark a spot 1¼" from the long edge and the short edge and drill a ½" hole.

3 Drill a ⁵⁄₁₆" hole, centered, the length of the spout. Draw a wavy line in from the two long edges and one short edge and cut along this line. Cut the undrilled mid tier and top tier pieces on a band saw to form the lip of each pool. Draw a wavy line around the perimeter of each, about ⅜" to ½" in from the edge.

4 On the mid tier, mark the waterfall line from a point 1" from the corner and extending 2" up the long side. On the top tier, mark a point ½" along a short side and 1" along the long side. Remove the center of each piece, cutting along the wavy line and using the waterfall area as the saw blade's entry point.

5 Cement together two sets of two vertical supports so you have a 1" thick piece 2⅜" tall. When fully dry, drill a ½" hole, centered, through the 2⅜" length of one.

6 Dry-fit the two short and two long sides on top of the base. When you are comfortable with the fit, apply epoxy cement to the bottom of one long edge and place the pieces in position. When dry, add epoxy to the vertical edges and the bottom of the short and long sides, then position the remaining pieces.

7 Cement the wavy-lip mid tier piece to its uncut base. Repeat for the top tier. Cement the corner support along the top short edge of the base in one corner. Cement the undrilled support to the bottom of the mid tier about 1½" in from one corner.

8 Place your pump in the base at the corner with the support. Dry-fit the mid tier over it, making sure that the hole lines up with the pump's hole. Apply cement to the bottom of the support and the top of the corner support and secure the mid tier in place, angling it either toward the center of the base pool area or squaring it to the edge.

9 Cement the drilled support over the hole in the mid tier. Cement the top tier onto the support. Cement the spout on to the top tier.

10 Drill two ¹⁄₁₆" holes ¼" into the bottom of each flamingo and cement 3" lengths of jewelry wire into them. Bend the wire as needed to create a natural pose, trimming off any excess wire. If you have trouble getting the flamingos to remain upright, drill ¹⁄₁₆" holes into the base and cement the wire in the holes.

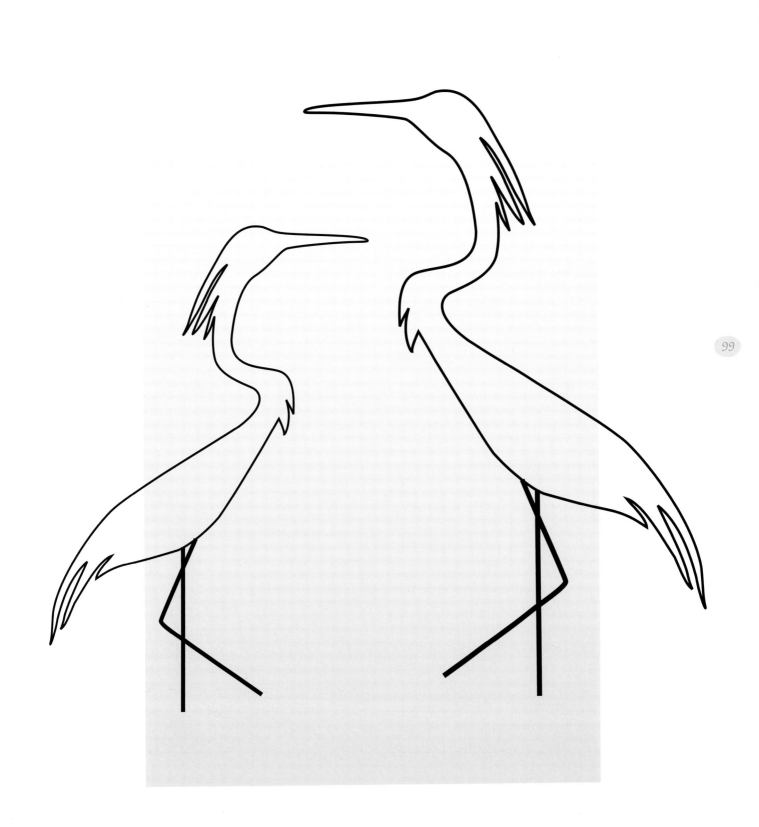

Bamboo Spout Fountain

The hollow space in bamboo canes makes the perfect cover-up for plastic tubing. To create an interesting water flow, marble squares were arranged like stair steps for a cascading effect.

MATERIALS
- Wide and narrow lengths of bamboo
- Hand saw
- Raffia
- 20" (50 cm) length of plastic tubing
- 90° elbow adapter (a good fit is essential so have your tubing with you when shopping for this part)
- Submersible pump
- Oblong basin
- 4 or 5 pieces of marble in different sizes
- Small white marble garden stones
- Water plants, optional

INSTRUCTIONS

1   Begin building the bamboo spout by cutting a piece of wide bamboo to the length of your container's height. Measure and mark a length of narrow bamboo two-thirds the length of the first piece and cut it at an angle. Cut a piece of plastic tubing to the length of each of these pieces plus 1".

2   Hold the unangled edge about ¾" (19 mm) down from one end of the wider bamboo and trace the narrow bamboo's shape with a pencil. Cut out an opening in the shape of your tracing, allowing a small amount of extra space on all sides for ease.

3   Cut two lengths of narrow bamboo to the length of your basin plus 2" (5 cm). Place the spout in between the two lengths about 5" (12 cm) in from one end. Tightly wrap the narrow bamboo strips together at both ends with raffia and tie off.

4 Gently lay the bamboo on top of your basin. Stand back and study the effect. Shorten any bamboo pieces that strike you as too long. Remove the spout piece and insert the plastic tubing up through the bottom. When the tubing reaches the top side hole, carefully connect one side of the elbow adaptor to the tubing. Connect the other side of the elbow adapter to the other length of tubing, then work the tubing through the narrow spout piece.

5 Slide the narrow spout piece over the tubing and gently into the hole. Secure with hot glue and cut off any tubing protruding through the angled end. Replace the spout unit back in place, retying the raffia if necessary.

6 Replace the spout unit over the basin. Trim the tubing and insert it into the pump. (Note: If you have an especially deep basin, you may need to elevate your pump on stacks of marble or on an unopened can of vegetables.) Set the pump's pressure on its lowest setting.

7 Fill the area around the pump with small marble stones, taking care not to block the pump's intake filters. Add water to your basin and plug in the pump. Stack the marble under the area where the water falls and play with different arrangements to create a cascading effect you find pleasing. Increase the water pressure if necessary.

8 If you choose to decorate the fountain with water plants, be sure to check the fountain frequently for plant debris to prevent the intake filters from becoming clogged.

Wood Basin Fountain

The natural beauty of a handcrafted wood basin makes a lovely frame for a tabletop fountain. You can purchase a wood basin in many garden centers (and a plastic liner to match), or you can make your own with the woodworking instructions on pages 104–107.

MATERIALS
- Wood basin and waterproof liner
- Submersible pump
- Plastic coupling
- Filler material (foam pipe insulation was used in this fountain), optional
- 5 pieces of slate, 5 at least an inch smaller on all sides than the basin and 1 approximately 3" (7 cm) wide (Note: you can purchase slate with predrilled holes as a kit in stores that carry a variety of fountain-making supplies.)
- Ceramic drill bits and drill
- Protective eyewear
- Miniature terra cotta pitcher
- Glue gun
- Garden stones, well washed and rinsed
- Air plant, decorative rocks, and a small piece of flat stone such as slate

102

INSTRUCTIONS

1 Prepare the coupling as directed on page 28. Set the pump on its lowest pressure setting and place it in the center of the basin. Place the coupling over the pump, taking extra care to make sure the electrical cord isn't crimped.

2 Cut pieces of foam pipe insulation to fit around the coupling. Rest the largest piece of slate on top of the coupling, taking care to align its hole with the pump's. Add the remaining pieces of slate, again taking care to align the holes. Note: You may need to move the pump to get the rocks in the position you want.

3 Hold the miniature pitcher on its side over the top rock; mark the spot where you'd like the water to come through. Drill a matching-size hole in the pitcher and hot glue it to the top rock with the holes aligned.

4 Add enough water to cover the pump's intake filters by more than an inch. Plug in the fountain and adjust the top rock for water flow and sound. The water should flow in a pleasing style without splashing on the top wood trim of the fountain. Adjust the water pressure if necessary. Fill the area around the outside of the coupling with stones.

5 To make the decorative accent on the side of the fountain, lightly glue the air plant to one side of the slate piece. Hot glue small crystals or stones near the base of the plant. Note: Be sure to wipe any water that spills or splashes on the wood trim or sides to avoid water spots. Apply a coat of paste wax every six

months to a year depending on use and water spillage. Careful care will result in a longer-lasting fountain.

Hand-Crafted Wood Basin

MATERIALS
- 4 pieces of select hardwood for the fountain body
- 4 pieces of select hardwood for the top trim
- 9" (22.5 cm) square of ⅛" (3 mm) pegboard
- Plexiglass liner box (you can build this from plexiglass slightly smaller than the fountain body frame)
- Sandpaper (80, 120, 160, and 220 grit)
- Waterproof wood glue
- Tung oil finish
- Masking tape
- 000 steel wool
- 100% clear waterproof silicone sealer
- Finishing wax
- 2 clean, dry cloths for waxing and polishing (old t-shirts work well)
- 5 small cork coasters
- 4 large cork coasters for fountain bottom

TOOLS
- Table saw
- Tabletop sander, orbital sander, palm sander (optional)
- Biscuit jointer (optional) and 4 #10 biscuits
- Miter saw
- Picture frame clamp or strap box clamp
- Hammer and small nails or staple gun
- Drill with masonry bits
- Protective eyewear

INSTRUCTIONS

1 Cut the four fountain side pieces to 10 x 3 x 1 (25 x 7.5 x 2.5 cm). Number the side of each piece to maintain the grain flow. Cut the four top trim pieces to 11½ x 1½ x ¼ (29 cm x 4 cm x 6 mm). Sand all eight side and top trim pieces to a smooth finish, first with 80 grit, then 120 grit, and then 160 grit.

2 Use a table saw to make a 45–degree cut to the four side pieces. This cut will allow the side pieces to form a box. Use a biscuit jointer to cut a biscuit joint in each of the four side pieces of the fountain. (This step is optional; you many use any type of joinery you wish.)

3 To assemble the sides of the box, lay the four pieces of the hardwood body out on a table with their flat sides up. Using the numbers on the side of each piece as a guide, lay them out so that the grain of the wood flows from one piece to the next. Turn the pieces of wood over so that the grooved (biscuit joint) side is now face up.

4 Put one or two small squirts of waterproof wood glue into each biscuit groove. Do not over-glue. Place one biscuit into every other groove so that each two joining pieces of wood have one biscuit. Starting at one end, bush the piece of wood with a biscuit into the next one without a biscuit. The biscuit should be going into the grooves that already have glue inside them. Do not add glue to the outside of the biscuits or to the sides of the wood pieces.

5 Use a picture frame clamp or a strap box clamp available at most hardware or home and builder supply stores to allow you to create a tight-fitting box without gaps on the corners. This is a very important step, so take your time. If you do end up with gaps, use natural wood putty to fill them in. Allow the box to dry for at least 24 hours.

6 To assemble the trim, use a miter saw to cut a 45–degree angle on each of the four top trim pieces to form a frame for the top of the fountain. The finished size of the trim pieces should be 11½ x 1½ x ¼.

7 If you have only one box or frame clamp, wait until your box has dried before starting this step. Lay the trim pieces in a square, flat on the table. Using masking tape, tape the four corners together so that you have a flat-looking picture frame. Turn the picture frame over so that the side without the tape is face up. Bending the frame in half so that two opposite corners open up, apply waterproof wood glue into the open seams.

8 Repeat the above process for the other two corners. Tape over the glued corners with masking tape and wipe up any excess glue. Carefully put the picture frame or box strap clamp around all four corners of the trim and tighten the clamp. Allow the trim to dry for 24 hours.

9 When both the box and trim pieces are dry, sand both structures separately with 220-grit sandpaper until you are satisfied with the results. Apply wood putty to fill in gaps at the corners and seams if necessary. Sand the sides at an angle to create a rounded look if desired.

10 Drill or cut a narrow groove approximately ⅛ to ¼" deep on the inside of one side of the finished box. This groove should run the width of the inside of the fountain, and will provide extra room to run the pump's electrical cord between the plexiglass liner and the fountain wall. Continue this groove on the bottom of the fountain and out the side.

11 To attach the body and the trim, lay the trim down on a flat work surface and apply glue to the top of the fountain body. (Do not over-glue.) Set the fountain body down onto the trim. Clamp the top trim piece to the body. Sandwich the fountain between two solid boards that are larger than the fountain. Clamp the two boards together. Be sure to clean up any glue that squeezes out. Allow to dry for at least 24 hours.

12 To seal the wooden parts of the fountain, apply a liberal amount of tung oil finish to the inside and outside of the entire fountain, following the manufacturer's instructions. Wipe dry after about 15 minutes. Repeat this process on the outside of the fountain top and sides a minimum of four to six times. The more coats of oil, the better. Use a fine 000 steel wool to apply the last coat of oil and polish the wood to a lustrous finish. Wipe dry and allow to cure for a minimum of 24 hours. This process may take several days.

13 Turn the fountain face down on a flat work surface. Apply clear, waterproof 100% silicone sealer to the inside top lip of the fountain to create a seal for the plexiglass liner.

14 Place the fountain pump inside the upside-down fountain box. Position the pump cord along the precut groove in one side of the fountain and up over the edge. Push the plexiglass liner down into the fountain box until it fits snugly against the trim frame and the silicone seal.

15 Place four of the small cork coasters onto the four corners of the plexiglass liner and one in the center. (The coasters will cushion the plexiglass liner from the bottom board and allow air to flow between the liner and the bottom of the box.)

16 Place the bottom board on the bottom of the fountain. Using small nails or a powerful stapler, nail the bottom board to the fountain base. Be sure the pump cord is allowed to pass through the groove and out the side of the bottom. Secure the four large cork

coasters on each corner of the bottom of the fountain. Turn the fountain over and wipe off any excess silicone seal that may have squeezed out around and inside the fountain trim.

17 After a minimum of 24 hours have passed since your last coat of tongue oil, apply the finishing wax by putting about a tablespoon of wax in a cloth (such as an old tee-shirt). Allow the wax to squeeze through the cloth as you rub the fountain. Wait about 15 to 20 minutes, then polish the fountain with a dry, smooth cloth or paper towel. Repeat this process after 24 hours if desired. (Be sure to review the manufacturer's instructions before beginning this step.)

18 Add a bead of the water-proof silicone seal to the coupling and place it over the pump and against the bottom of the plexiglass liner. Allow to dry for 24 hours. Finish assembling the fountain as directed on page 104.

SHIPPING A FOUNTAIN

You've made a great fountain that will make a great gift for your favorite relative. Just one problem: She lives in the Canadian Alps—and you don't. Actually, shipping a fountain isn't such a problem if you follow a few simple guidelines.

First, take a photo of the completed fountain and send it along so she'll have a good idea of how your gift will look once she reassembles it!

Locate a sturdy box and lots of packing peanuts. Empty all water from the fountain, wipe off any remaining water, and give it a day or two to completely dry out.

If it's critical that your pump be placed in a precise location, then mark the spot with a few dots of colorful fingernail polish or secure the pump in place in your basin with electrical tape.

Partially fill the box with packing material. Wrap your basin well with newspaper, place it on top of the packing material, and add another layer of packing material on top of it. If you didn't tape your pump in place, wrap it carefully with newspaper and layer it on top of the basin.

If you have multiple remaining parts to your fountain, label them on their underside with masking tape to guide the receiver while assembling. (For instance, the fountain on page 56 was marked bottom left, top right, etc, for assembly guidance.) Wrap up any remaining elements in newspaper and carefully place in the box.

If your fountain uses stones or marbles to disguise the mechanics, place them in a sealable plastic bag and layer them in the box with packing material.

Plan to spend a few minutes on the phone talking your fountain's new owner through the assembly process.

Flower Vase Fountain

Here's an impromptu, ten-minute fountain to make from your favorite flower vase. For easier access to the pump, place the pump on top of a tall can instead of at the bottom of the vase.

MATERIALS
- Tall flower vase
- Soda or juice can (unopened)
- Submersible pump
- Large stones (won't be seen in the finished fountain)
- Tumbled glass pieces

INSTRUCTIONS

1 Place the can in the center of the vase. Set the pump on its lowest pressure setting and place it on top of the can. Loosely fill the area around and on top of the can with stones, taking care not to block the pump's intake filters.

2 Fill the vase with water and turn on the pump. Make any necessary adjustments in pressure, then cover the rocks with a layer of tumbled glass pieces. Note: You can reduce the water flow from a geyser to a gurgle by covering the outtake hole with tumbled glass.

DESIGNER:

Sherry Feldman

Water Garden Fountain

Silk flowers and foliage are a great choice for tabletop fountains. Many of the newer types look very natural and their decay debris will never clog up your pump's filter.

MATERIALS

- Bowl
- Submersible pump
- 3" (7.5 cm) length of plastic tubing
- Light switch plate
- Stems of silk foliage and blooms
- Ceramic frog or turtle
- Silk butterfly

INSTRUCTIONS

1 Set the pump on its lowest pressure setting and place it in the center of your bowl. Insert the plastic tubing, then lower the light switch plate over and down the tubing until it rests on the pump.

2 Arrange several stems of silk foliage and blooms around one side of the fountain and place the frog on the adjacent side. Fill the bowl with enough water to cover the pump's intake filters by more than an inch (2.5 cm).

3 Plug in the pump and make any necessary adjustments in water flow by changing the pressure setting or trimming the tubing length. Disguise the tubing by placing a single leaf in front of it, then position the silk butterfly among the foliage.

Watering Can Fountain

This simple fountain can be made in virtually any size, from extra large to miniature. Find a charming watering can first, then search out a basin in a well-proportioned size.

MATERIALS
- Watering can
- Spray paint, optional
- Drill and metal drill bits
- Protective eyewear
- Mounting brackets or adhesive
- Basin or bowl
- Submersible pump
- Plastic tubing about 2" (5 cm) longer than the can's spout
- Handful of attractive rocks or stones
- Several silk leaves

INSTRUCTIONS

1 Spray paint the watering can if necessary. After the paint has completely dried, turn the can upside down and mark the spot where you anticipate the tubing will exit from the spout. Drill a ⅝" (15 mm) hole in that location.

2 Thread the tubing in through the spout end of the can and out through your drilled hole. Hold the watering can against the rim of your basin and play with different placements. Set the pump's pressure to its lowest setting and place it under the can on the side of the basin. Insert the tubing into the pump, fill the basin with water, and plug in the pump. If necessary, change the water flow by changing the placement of the can.

3 Mount the watering can in place using adhesive or brackets. (Alternately, rest the side of the can against a wall or build up a support system from underneath with rocks.) Adjust the water pressure as necessary and float several silk leaves on the water's surface. Add several rocks to the bottom of the basin.

DESIGNER:

Dawn Cusick

Tulip Water Flow Fountain

A wonderful array of special water flow effects can be created with fountain head attachments. Be sure to measure the width of the water spray in your kitchen sink before choosing a container.

MATERIALS
- Submersible pump
- 7" (18 cm) length of plastic tubing
- Basin or bowl at least 6" (15 cm) larger than the width of the water spray
- Decorative garden pot about the same width as the water spray
- Fountain head attachment
- Decorative stones or rocks

INSTRUCTIONS

1 Set the pump on its lowest pressure setting and place it in the center of the large bowl. Insert the tubing into the pump. Thread the tubing through the hole in the garden pot and lower the pot until it rests on the pump. Ideally, the bottom of the pot should be at the same height or just a little lower than the rim of the large bowl. (You may need to rest the pump on a can of vegetables to achieve the correct height; if so, securing the two elements together with electrical tape, taking care not to block the intake filters, can add stability.)

2 Trim the tubing down to ½" (13 mm) below the rim of the pot, then attach the fountain head to the tubing. You may need to wrap the connecting area with electrical tape or add a tubing coupling to achieve a snug fit. Add enough water to cover the pump's intake filters by more than an inch (2.5 cm) and plug in the pump. Make any necessary adjustments in the pump's pressure.

3 Drain out some of the water and begin filling the space around the pump with large rocks or stones. Refill the bowl with water and enjoy.

DESIGNERS:

Chris Rankin

and

Susan Kieffer

Lantern Fountain

When you tire of making simple bowl fountains, try your hand at building a custom fountain from recycled materials. This fountain was inspired by an antique oil lantern found in a secondhand shop.

MATERIALS

- Oil lantern with glass shade removed
- Drill and metal bits
- Protective eyewear
- 10" (25 cm) length of plastic tubing
- Brass or silver basin
- Submersible pump

INSTRUCTIONS

1 Clean the inside of the lantern to remove any remaining oil. Drill a ½" (13 mm) hole in the bottom center of the lantern. Thread the plastic tubing in through the bottom of the lantern and out through the space normally occupied by the wick.

2 Set the pump on its lowest pressure setting and place it in the bottom of the basin so that the pump's hole is centered within the basin. Insert the tubing into the pump and add enough water to cover the intake filters by at least an inch (2.5 cm).

3 Plug in the fountain and make any necessary adjustments in the pressure. A high-pressure setting should give you a gurgling water flow just above the top of the lantern. A lower pressure setting, on the other hand, will allow the water to first fill the reservoir at the top of the lantern and then spill over the sides.

Dry Stack Fountain

The water flow in this fountain creates a self-misting refuge for moisture-loving house plants. Experiment with different lengths of plastic tubing to create a variety of water flows. Cutting the tubing just below the top rock level causes the water to "jump" out of the hole, while cutting the tubing an inch or so lower creates a gurgling effect.

MATERIALS
- Large terra cotta rimmed pot
- Bowl to fit inside rimmed pot
- 4" (10 cm) coupling
- Submersible pump
- Piece of slate about the same size as the shallow bowl
- Drill and masonry bits
- Protective eyewear
- Interesting assortment of small rocks, some of them with flat surfaces
- Epoxy or other suitable adhesive
- 15" (37 cm) length of plastic tubing
- Potting soil
- House plants

INSTRUCTIONS

1 Prepare the coupling as directed on page 28. Set the pump on its highest pressure setting and place it in the center of the bowl. Place the coupling over the pump, taking care to position the electrical cord under one of the holes.

2 Drill a hole just a little larger than your tubing in the center of the slate. Build a rock pyramid around the hole in the slate, taking care to keep a gap in the center for the tubing.

3 Add enough water to the bowl to cover the pump's intake filters by more than an inch (2.5 cm). Insert the tubing into the pump and then lower the rock structure over the tubing until it rests flat on the coupling.

4 Plug in the pump and adjust the pressure setting and tube length to create the desired water flow.

5 Lower the rimmed pot over the fountain and fill the space with potting soil and plants.

119

Concrete and Mirror Fall

The popularity of concrete as a design material continues to increase as contemporary crafters and artists in many fields discover the versatility and ease of working with today's concrete blends. This piece was poured from a concrete-vermiculite blend that is light weight and easy to embellish with textured patterns.

MATERIALS

- Large circular item for mold (a wooden barrel ring was used by this designer)
- Sheet of plywood at least a few inches larger than your mold
- 8" (20 cm) square mirror
- Empty coffee can
- 2 coat hangers or metal rods
- Large plastic bucket
- Portland cement
- Vermiculite or other concrete aggregate
- 20" (50 cm) length of copper tubing
- Old butter knife or metal nail file
- Rectangular cardboard box about the size you'd like your finished basin to be
- Second rectangular box, about an inch smaller on all sides than the first one
- Concrete sealant
- Submersible pump
- 24" (61 cm) length of plastic tubing

INSTRUCTIONS

1 Place your mold on top of the plywood. Position the mirror near the top and place an empty coffee can in the center of the mirror. Mix six parts portland cement to six parts vermiculite to one part water and stir until you have a firm but soupy consistency. Pour the mixture into the mold and around the outside of the coffee can until it's about 2" (5 cm) high. Sink coat hangers or metal rods into the middle of the concrete for strength.

3 Remove the mold and the coffee can when the concrete is firm but still moist. Press a curved length of copper tubing into the moist concrete, echoing the shape of the mirror. Add textural patterns by sculpting with a butter knife or metal nail file while the concrete is still moist. Carve out a shallow, circular recess around the mirror. Working from the back side, carve a small hole slightly larger than the tubing near the center back of the recess.

4 Place your larger box on a flat surface and pour 2" of the concrete mixture into it. Place your smaller box on top of the wet concrete, centering it so that there's an equal amount of space on all sides. Pour cement in the areas between the two boxes to form the basin's walls. Allow the concrete to harden, then peel off the cardboard. Add several coats of concrete sealant to the inside of the basin as directed by the manufacturer's instructions.

5 Position the mirrored concrete form toward the front of the basin. Set the pump on its highest pressure setting and place it in the center back of the basin. Insert the tubing into the hole and into the pump, trimming off any excess length. Add enough water to the basin to cover the pump's intake filters by more than an inch. Plug in the pump and make any necessary adjustments in the pressure setting.

121

Copper and Marble Fall

Marble, glass, and copper make a handsome combination in this fountain designed to showcase a vertical water fall. The pump sits in the basin, behind the marble, while the tubing carries water up the back side of the marble.

MATERIALS

- Pipe cutter
- 28" (71 cm) length of 1" (2.5 cm) copper pipe
- 30" (76 cm) length of ½" (13 mm) copper pipe (purchase extra pipe if you've never soldered before
- 000 sand paper
- 4½ x 13" (11.5 x 33 cm) piece of polished marble, split at an angle*
- Plumbing solder
- Propane torch
- Flux and small brush
- 4½ x 13" mirror
- Epoxy
- Submersible pump
- 13" length of plastic tubing
- Rectangular copper basin at least 6" (15 cm) wide
- Electrical tape

*Note: Don't obsess about finding a marble slab exactly this size; just find a piece you like and alter the instructions below to suit your marble's measurements.

INSTRUCTIONS

1 Cut the 1" pipe into two 14" (30 cm) lengths. Cut the ½" pipe into eight 1½ (5 cm) lengths and four 4½" (11.5 cm) lengths. Sand all pieces.

2 Review and practice the soldering techniques described on page 124. Solder one 1½" piece of pipe to the top and bottom sides of both 14" pipe lengths.

3 Place the two 14" lengths upside down and place the marble slabs over them, making sure the marble is flush with the top and bottom ends of the piping and leaving a gap in the middle.

4 Solder a 4½" pipe length to all four corners, positioning it flush with the top of the marble and the other pipe pieces.

5 Repeat step 2 with the remaining 1½" pipe lengths to create a secure casing for the marble.

6 Set the pump on its lowest pressure setting and place it in the center of the basin against one long wall. Insert the tubing into the pump.

7 Secure the mirror to the back side of the copper/marble assembly with epoxy and allow to completely dry.

8 Stand the copper/marble assembly upright in front of the pump. Brace the assembly if necessary with a few rocks.

122

9 Fill the basin with enough water to cover the pump's intake filters by more than an inch. Tape the tubing in place against the top back side of the mirror about an inch (2.5 cm) down from the top. Hold the tubing over the front side of the marble and plug in the pump. Unplug the pump.

10 rim the tubing at a slight angle so that the side closest to the marble is flush with the top of the marble and the back side of the tubing is slightly higher. (The goal is to get as much of the water as possible to spill down the front side of the marble without the tubing being too prominent to the casual observer.)

Quick Soldering Lesson
For Copper and Marble Fall
On page 123

All of the materials necessary for copper soldering can be found in the plumbing section of any hardware store. Sweating copper pipes (welding two pieces together) requires five things: a small propane torch, plumbing solder, a binding agent called flux, fine sand paper, and a small brush.

Begin by sanding the copper to clean the surface and create grooves for the solder. Apply flux paste with a brush in only the areas you want the solder to stick. Light the torch and apply direct heat to your copper soldering joint for 30 seconds to several minutes. While the joint is heating up, place your pluming solder wire directly on the spot you want to join. DO NOT apply torch flame directly to the solder. (The solder has to melt onto the copper for it to bond well, so always heat the joint and not the solder.) If your solder beads up without melting into the joint, the joint has probably not been heated enough (or you forgot to add the flux). Generous with the flux and light with the solder is logic to live by.

If you've never soldered before, purchase some extra pipe and make several practice sweats before you begin working on the project.

124

Office Desk Fountain

Bring the calming presence of water to your home or business office in a recycled computer monitor. The water cascades down a series of stair-stepped CDs.

MATERIALS
- Discarded computer monitor
- Drill and metal bits
- Clear, waterproof silicone caulk
- Roll of clear 2" (5 cm) packing tape
- 31 CDs (blanks or discards are fine)
- Epoxy or strong adhesive
- Pliers
- 6-tool pegboard rack
- Wire cutters
- Heavy-gauge jewelry wire
- 2 dozen clothespins
- 16" (40 cm) length of plastic tubing
- Submersible pump
- Battery-powered closet light (optional)
- Large plastic bowl with lid

INSTRUCTIONS

1 Bring your old monitor to a computer repair shop and ask them to remove all of the electrical components. (Although you can do this step yourself, the condenser can store enough electrical energy to cause electrical shock.)

2   Drill several ½" (13 mm) holes close to each other in the bottom center of the monitor. Caulk and tape the interior of the monitor (except for the drilled holes). Allow the caulk to dry at least 12 hours, then fill the monitor with water and check for leaks. Caulk and tape again if necessary.

3   Glue the CDs together in pairs with their shiny side facing out and allow them to dry for at least 12 hours.

4   Drill a ⁵⁄₁₆" (9 mm) hole near the outside edge in five of the CD pairs. Drill two ⁵⁄₁₆" holes about an inch (2.5 cm) apart along the outside edge of the single CD.

5   Using heavy pliers, remove the right-angle ends (the area which would normally fit into the holes on the pegboard) of the pegboard tool rack. Cut the loops in half on one end of the rack with wire cutters. Cut six lengths of wire, each measuring 4" (10 cm).

6   Attach the 5 drilled CD pairs to the areas between the loops of the rack by threading a wire length through the hole and then twisting it around the peg rack. Glue a CD pair to the center top of each CD that's attached to the rack, creating a stair-step pattern as you work. Secure each CD pair in place with a clothespin for 12 hours while the adhesive dries.

7   Use the remaining piece of jewelry wire to attach the two-hole single CD to the inside top back corner of the monitor, centering it from right to left and passing the wire through vents in the plastic. (If the vents aren't

in a suitable position, drill the necessary holes through this portion of the monitor to accommodate the wires.)

8   Drill a hole slightly larger than your tubing in the center back of the monitor just below the CD. Thread the tubing through this hole and then through the hole in the CD. Tape the tubing against the outside of the monitor.

9   Mount the rack inside the monitor by pulling up on the CD that's wired inside the monitor and hooking the cut loops onto the edge of that CD. The bottom piece of the rack should rest on some portion of the floor of the monitor. Mount the battery-powered light (if desired) inside the top of the monitor.

10   Drill or cut a 2" (5 cm) hole in the center of the bowl's lid. Use a ½" drill bit to drill two holes about ½" apart in the upper edge of the bowl. Cut through the edges of one of the holes.

11   Set the pump on its highest pressure setting and center it in the bottom of the bowl. Open the cut edges of the hole you made in step 10 and place the pump's electrical cord in the hole. Thread the plastic tubing into the bowl through the remaining hole and insert it in the pump.

12   Fill the bowl with enough water to cover the pump's intake filters by more than an inch. Secure the lid in place and align the monitor's base holes over the hole in the lid. Plug in the pump and adjust the CD rack to improve the water flow if necessary.

Contributing Designers

EVANS R. CARTER is a college student living in Asheville, North Carolina. She describes herself as a "Jane-of-all-trades who enjoys working with metal, wood, stone, glass, paint, and just about everything else."

PERRI CRUTCHER, for years a professional floral designer and stylist in Paris and New York City, produces elegant floral creations at Perri, Ltd., his equally elegant floral decor studio in Asheville, North Carolina.

LEE DAVIS holds an MFA degree in pottery from Indiana University. He taught at Kansas State University, Mary Baldwin College, Stuart Hall, and the Campbell Folk School before opening Birdfoot Ridge, a full-time studio located near Lee's home in Brasstown, North Carolina.

TIMOTHY M. DENBO owns and operates Nature's Melody, a tabletop water fountain studio in Ashland, Oregon. Timothy's fountains vary in design and material, from the casual glass and ceramics to lustrous, handmade solid hardwood fountains. His company also carries mail order supplies for the do-it-yourselfer.

SHERRY FELDMAN enjoys virtually every type of crafting, from ceramics to painting to fountain making. She divides her time between the Florida sunshine and the North Carolina mountains.

DANA IRWIN is a graphic artist and illustrator who designs books (and occasionally makes projects for them). She lives in Asheville, North Carolina, and spends her spare time dancing and gardening.

SUSAN KIEFFER is a former women's clothing designer, travel newswriter, and television camerawoman. She has dabbled in crafts all of her life and currently works for Lark Books Catalog. She lived in the Florida Keys for many years, but traded the sea for the mountains of Asheville, North Carolina.

SUSAN KINNEY is an interior designer living in Asheville, North Carolina. She specializes inboth residential and commercial interior design as well as an eclectic array of jewelry, fashion items, and accessories for the home and garden. She can be reached at designdr@mindspring.com.

JEAN WALL PENLAND is an artist who paints and teaches in the mountains of North Carolina. She has received an Adolph and Esther Gottlieb Foundation grant and a Pollock-Krasner Foundation grant.

SUZANNE MCCALL, a resident of Hollister, California, is the Fountain Goddess. After years as an interior home designer, Suzanne started a fountain business specializing in custom-order, personally designed fountains that bring calmness and good luck. Her work can be viewed on her website at www.fountain-goddess.com.

JAMES TRUE is a creationist specializing in the second and third dimensions. His graphic designs and sculptures can be seen all over Western North Carolina. Visitors are welcome at his home gallery. Email him at true@katuah.com.

JACK WALL likes making just about any type of art out of Corien matter (solid surface countertop); a sampling of his designs can be seen on his web site at www.walpen.com. He lives in Asheville, North Carolina.

CARLTON WHATLEY was born and raised in South Texas. His past careers include photography and nursing. He is currently an independent computer consultant living in Asheville, North Carolina.

Index

A

Acoustics, water, 34
Adapters
    T-flow, 87
    Tulip, 114
Airplants, 21

B

Bamboo, 101
Basins
    Types of, 16
    Waterproofing, 25
Baskets, 50
Bowls
    Types of, 16
    Waterproofing, 25
Brass, 58, 71
Building basics, 22-24, 29-31

C

Concealing pumps and tubing, 18-21
Containers
    Types of, 16
    Waterproofing, 25
Corian, 92, 97
Couplings, 27, 28

D

Design accents, 18-21
Drills, 26, 27
Drip loops, 35

G

Glass chips, 20

I

Inspiration, 18

M

Maintenance, 36, 37
Marbles, 20
Mosaic chips, 75

P

Plants, 21
Pumps, 14, 15
Pyramids, 78

R

Rocks, 19, 20

S

Safety, 35
Shells, 60
Slate, 19, 20
Stones, 19, 20

T

Tile, 44
Tubing, 15, 27

V

Vases, 58, 108

W

Water
    Acoustics, 34
    Flow, 34
    Levels, 36
    pH, 17
Waterproofing, 25